Disrupting the African Mindset

Blackstone Books

Blackstone Books, an imprint of the WPI Press, publishes engaging, idea-driven books for a global audience, covering a wide range of topics, perspectives, and voices.

Guided by our mission to inform, clarify, inspire, and entertain, the Blackstone Books imprint acts as a catalyst for bringing big ideas to new audiences and encouraging life-long learning while contributing to the public discourse of the time.

Blackstone Books welcomes contributions that complement these goals from both academic and non-academic authors.

Disrupting the African Mindset

From Divided to United

Adu Opoku-Boahin

BLACK
STONE
BOOKS

An imprint of the
Worcester Polytechnic Institute Press
Worcester, Massachusetts

First edition published 2026 by Blackstone Books, an imprint of the Worcester Polytechnic Institute Press

The WPI Press
100 Institute Road
Worcester, MA 01609

Cataloging-in-Publication Data
Name: Opoku-Boahin, Adu, author.
Title: Disrupting the African Mindset: From Divided to United / Adu Opoku-Boahin.
Description: Worcester, MA: The WPI Press, 2026 | Includes appendices and index.
Identifiers: ISBN: 978-1-965358-09-2 (paperback) | ISBN: 978-1-965358-10-8 (PDF) | ISBN: 978-1-965358-11-5 (epub)
Subjects: Africa—Politics and government—21st century | Africa—Economic integration | Pan-Africanism | Africa—Social conditions—21st century

"The path will not be fully clear, yet we must have the vision to move forward.

The path will not be easy, yet we must start with practical solutions.

The path will be littered with obstacles, yet we must be prepared to navigate towards our goal.

The path will instill fear, yet we must find our courage."

—Adu Opoku-Boahin, 2025

CONTENTS

Preface

LET'S SOLVE PROBLEMS

I am a problem solver, a strategist by trade, and like so many people who solve problems, I see opportunities for problem solving everywhere. How might I help? What can I bring? What else is required? Can I achieve impact? Why get involved?

My personal aspirations are simply that I love Africa, my motherland, my home, and I want to help Africa. I want to see Africa develop, grow, and prosper. I love solving the problems of the world's biggest companies by day, but by night I ponder a bigger, more important problem: a divided Africa.

It's not just that Africa is divided, in conflict, underdeveloped, poor, held in debt, exploited. It's that it needn't be this way, that it's possible to end the conflict, poverty, and indebtedness, to develop, and to unite.

As such, the problem shifts. The problem is not that Africa has problems; it's that Africa isn't fixing its problems, even though it has a wealth of natural resources and amazing people. So why not? Why can't Africa seem to move forward to take its place on the world stage—to harness its resources and leverage and support its people? What else is needed? What's the policy intervention required? Or should we ask, "What's the strategy?"

I am not a politician. And while I have a deep interest in policy, I believe policy, in particular politics, is part of the problem for Africa. Politics is ideology. It may drive change but is clouded by ideology—a singular way of thinking that cannot take in rational cold hard data, analyses of develop reasoned arguments, or balanced solutions. By its very nature it is not strategic.

My experience in solving complex problems for global companies means I've honed my own strategic mindset, which I believe is important to any sort of problem solving. I think strategy is more useful to Africa than political ambition because it brings with it a totally different approach. A strategic mindset, in my opinion, is perhaps stronger and more useful than a political one, as it isn't fixed in place by ideology. Also, it isn't personal or about personality. It isn't about me or you. A strategic approach is simply about discovering, understanding, and then grasping opportunity. It's about us all.

WHY WRITE THIS BOOK?

I was born in Africa, raised in Austria, and now live in the United States, working more and more with policymakers in Africa, and this journey has given me a unique perspective on both the potential and the challenges of the African continent. The rich and diverse cultures, combined with seemingly endless natural resources and a young, vibrant population, position Africa to be on the cusp of a transformative era. Despite these immense assets, the continent has struggled with structural issues that hinder its development. My career as a global business leader, solving complex problems and creating opportunities for some of the world's most forward-thinking organizations, has equipped me with a set of skills and perspectives that I am now eager to apply to my natural homeland.

In order to eradicate poverty, I need to share my problems-solving capabilities, my ideas, and my time. I believe that my journey so far has equipped me to do just that effectively, and to achieve my goal.

Reflecting on my educational journey, which took me from Austria to the United States, I often ponder whether I would have had similar professional and educational opportunities if I had grown up in Ghana. The disparity in educational systems and access to resources between different parts of the world, including Ghana and Western countries like Austria and the US, is significant and likely would have impacted my path and the nature of my opportunities. Ghana, like many African countries, faces numerous challenges in its education sector, including limited funding, inadequate infrastructure, and a shortage of educational materials and qualified teachers. On the other hand, growing up in Ghana could have offered distinct advantages and opportunities. Ghana has a rich cultural heritage and a strong sense of community and resilience that deeply influences its educational approaches. These values could have instilled in me a different set of skills and perspectives, deeply rooted in local knowledge and practices, which are equally valuable but perhaps under-recognized in global business context.

The entrepreneurial spirit that pervades many African communities, driven by necessity and innovation, could have propelled me into early practical business experiences, providing a unique foundation that formal education sometimes lacks. The challenges themselves, while potentially limiting in some respects, could have also fostered a heightened sense of determination, adaptability, and creativity, crucial qualities in any field. While I undoubtedly missed out on many positives of growing up in Africa, I believe I am now able to bring back expertise and help a new generation of Africans to unlock opportunity. I am keen that by introducing more equitable educational practices and resources in Africa we can unlock potential, allowing more young Africans to access the same level of opportunities, regardless of where they grow up.

While considering my own journey, I also consider the journey of Africa. Africa's journey has been one of both profound triumphs and enduring challenges. Since Ghana marked its territory as the first sub-Saharan African country to gain independence almost sixty-eight years ago, the continent has undergone significant political, social, and economic changes. Each of these relatively recent milestones reflects a chapter in the broader narrative of resilience and aspiration. Yet, that aspiration, the full promise of Africa, remains unfulfilled, shackled by outdated models of leadership and governance that stifle innovation and suppress the voices of its most important resource: its people.

One of the central themes of this book is for Africa to truly realize its potential, which requires a fundamental rethinking of the concept of leadership. Traditional top-down leadership models must be inverted to empower a new generation of Africans. Young people, especially, need better education and more opportunities to participate actively in shaping policy, strategy, and development. They must be given the tools and platforms to contribute meaningfully to their societies and to the continent's destiny.

This book is not just an exploration of ideas but a call to action. It aims to challenge entrenched perceptions, inspire new thinking, and catalyze change. I delve into the art of the possible, a reimagination of what Africa could become if it harnesses its collective strengths and addresses its systemic challenges head on.

In looking toward to Africa's future, it is instructive to consider examples from elsewhere. The United Arab Emirates, for instance, has leveraged its oil wealth not merely to sustain its economy but to transform it, creating a world-class destination renowned for innovation and luxury. There are lessons here for Africa, particularly in how a clear vision and strategic investment can radically alter the global standing of a region. After we look at lessons from elsewhere, I focus firmly on Africa with my vision for the future.

Central to this book are the "necessary pivots," a visionary change agenda for a united Africa, enabled by technology, innovation, and a skilled workforce. These pivots are framed through a series of speculative questions that challenge the status quo and imagine a radically different future:

- Where is Africa's Schengen—and what if Africa was the United Countries of Africa, with a single currency and open borders?
- What might integration look like—and what if Africa had unified defense, health care, education and communication systems?
- What might self-sufficiency look like—and what if Africa's industries were more diverse, and what if Africa had better terms from the IMF?

> *Each of these questions opens a dialogue about the potential for structural and systemic reform. They prompt us to consider the benefits of deeper integration and cooperation across African states, not just economically, but politically and socially.*

As we look toward 2050, this book sets forth a series of aspirations for Africa's future. It is a future when the boundaries of what is possible are continually expanding. By 2050, I hope to see an Africa that is not merely participating in the global economy but is a leading force in it. An Africa where innovation is commonplace and opportunities are abundant, an Africa where every individual can pursue their dreams unencumbered by the legacy of colonialism or the shackles of poor governance, corruption, the threat of neocolonialism via foreign investment or simply a lack of ambition.

I read a lot, especially about my favorite topic of how to help Africa and Africans prosper. There are many leading thinkers who are deeply involved in the subject and many leaders with strong voices advocating for change. The challenges facing Africa are often made academic: explored, studied, quantified, pontificated over. There is much to be read about Africa, its history and future, much to be read about its problems. Yet there is less to be read of practical solutions to help Africa develop. In my view, there is lack of tangible and practical solutions. I want to change that. I want to offer those solutions.

This book is both a reflection of my journey and a roadmap for the future. It is a personal mission, born from a life lived between continents and cultures, and a professional manifesto, shaped by years of leadership and innovation. Join me as we explore the possibilities, engage with dynamic leaders, and take active steps toward a transformative future for Africa. Together, we can create a continent that thrives on equality, innovation, and prosperity—a truly unified Africa.

MY LIFE'S PURPOSE: ELIMINATING POVERTY

Poverty is not just an economic condition; it is a systemic failure, and as I discuss throughout this book, it is a paradox that in

Africa, a continent so rich in natural resources, innovation, and human potential, there exists both extreme wealth and extreme poverty. The stark contrast is neither natural nor sustainable. Nor is it acceptable, not to me at least.

I have never experienced poverty firsthand. It was not through my own hard work that I was born into a middle-class family in a comfortable city in Europe, offered a free education and health care, and nurtured to thrive by loving parents and a supportive community. I did not earn this opportunity. I was just lucky, just as millions of Africans who are born into poverty did not deserve their fate of growing up without education, health care, peace, opportunity, and in some cases without food and the basic resources to survive. They were just unlucky.

Now, as someone who knows he is lucky, and who's grasped those lucky opportunities with both hands, I know it's my turn to give back, to look around, to see what needs to be done and to create the opportunity for others—for everyone.

Africa's vast mineral wealth, fertile land, and young, ambitious population should be enough to guarantee prosperity for all, yet poverty remains rampant. Wealth is concentrated in the hands of very few, often at the expense of the many. Those at the bottom are left without the means to uplift themselves.

And yet, my strategy for ending poverty might surprise you. I don't want to advocate wealth redistribution, whereby those with wealth are forced to give it up to fund the poor. Why? Because there's no need. My vision for ending poverty is one of abundance, not one of lack. I know this strategy will work because I know there's more than enough to go around, and we don't need to compete for these resources, actually.

We can create a balanced society in which economic opportunities are widespread, in which entrepreneurship thrives, and in which technology enables progress for all; technology, after all, is the greatest equalizer of our time. In this book, I will talk about harnessing technology to aid development and unite Africa by accelerating financial inclusion through digital banking; moving government systems to the blockchain to ensure transparency and accountability; developing e-learning platforms and skills farms; and accelerating health care through advanced AI.

One question I am asked as a strategist is "How do you know which idea will work?" It's a valid question, and you might answer with a shrug and say it's all down to knowledge and experience: "the smarts." But today we actually do have a new weapon in our arsenal, a new tool of the trade. Now, even when it comes to predicting how best to end poverty, we have data. AI can be used to predict which development projects will return the most on their investment, which regions in Africa or any developing country will benefit most from infrastructure investments, and which sectors should be developed in which order to drive maximum impact. We can end the need for good luck.

Achieving my life's purpose of eliminating poverty is indeed possible. We have the resources in abundance, and now we have a way to know how best to leverage them, plus we have the ability to create systems that will enable us to measure and hone our efforts year over year until we get really good at it.

The time for action is now. The question is not whether poverty can be eradicated but whether we have the will to use the tools available to us to make it happen. I know we have the ability. I believe we have the will. We just need to determine where to end it first. I intend to dedicate my life to this cause.

HERE IS MY TAKE: THE 2050 AFRICA VISION

It's 2050 and I'm in Africa, but not as we know it today. Not yet at least. Since 2025, the continent has made a great shift and has leveraged its resources to fully realize its potential and take its place on the world stage. Bold decisions have been made, risks have been taken, and riches have indeed been won. My day begins at sunrise in Accra, Ghana, a thriving epicenter in a united African state. From my home office overlooking the bustling cityscape, I attend a virtual strategy meeting with my executive team distributed across Nairobi, Lagos, and Johannesburg as well as Zurich, Boston, Dubai, and London. Seamless connectivity is enabled through a continent-wide information system, allowing for efficient real-time data integration across all our operations.

My focus today is on supporting a global client with skilled African knowledge workers. The diversity of our team, reflective of Africa's commitment to inclusivity and diversity, brings a rich variety of perspectives that drive our mission forward effectively and enable our team to operate on an equal footing and on equal pay with global peers.

After a productive working session, I take a high-speed train to Lagos, Nigeria, where many of my global business clients are located. My UCoA (United Countries of Africa) passport allows me to easily cross borders, enhancing my ability to work fluidly across the continent. As part of my work in Nigeria, I work with business leaders to discuss and influence policies that support the growth of the education sector, improving the state education for all Africans.

Later in the afternoon, I visit one of my client's manufacturing sites in a newly developed area. I am shown their latest AI-driven systems, developed by brilliant minds nurtured by our continent-wide education system. Observing these young engineers, I am immensely proud of how they've applied their skills to crucial sectors within our booming economy. The teams here have developed their abilities; the companies have doubled down on building efficiencies to ensure they can operate at scale. They learned from the successes of others, they adopted a winning mindset, and they took ownership and showed true leadership. Now, Africa has its own infrastructure, infrastructure built by, owned by, and controlled by Africans.

By evening, I am back in Accra, participating in a community event aimed at empowering young entrepreneurs, with a focus on promoting leadership roles for women. Much has already been done to support women in leadership, and women already hold many roles in government. This event is to celebrate how far we've come and how far ahead we are in this regard. For me, this is about my deep commitment to nurturing the next generation of African leaders. The women in leadership roles over the last twenty-five years have ensured that true leadership has been embedded at every level of government and community and that everyone has had the chance to participate in their own development, in Africa's development.

At the end of a normal day in an extraordinary land, I am grateful for the sophisticated systems that support such harmonious work and life. In this unified Africa, we've realized a vision of connectivity, empowerment, and equity, establishing our continent as a beacon of progress and prosperity on the global stage. This not only elevates Africa economically but also enriches my life with purpose and pride. This vision would enrich the lives of 1.5 billion people.

In my vision, this united Africa operates efficiently. It is supported by integrated policies that foster economic growth and societal well-being. It is a continent where prosperity is widespread, societies support each other robustly, and global influence is marked by cooperation and innovation. It is a society in which political leaders are trusted and respected because they have done the right thing, kept their social contract, and led with humility for the benefit of all Africans. This scenario does not merely lift Africa; a prosperous Africa is a more prosperous world.

On the Road to 2050

The truth is this vision is far off, but it is not out of reach. It is not fanciful or frivolous. It is reasonable to assume that if nations, a continent even, is developing, that it can develop sufficiently to provide the necessary infrastructure and connectivity, to provide the relevant education and health care, that it can govern and organize to trade openly and support growth and prosperity. It is reasonable, is it not?

Let's look at what my vision takes. In the scenario in which Africa operates as one unified entity, the continent would need to function under a federal system similar to that of the United States or the European Union, with "country states" retaining significant autonomy while adhering to a central government. The government, consisting of members of the individual sovereign nations, oversees continental policies on foreign affairs, defense, monetary policy, and critical infrastructures such as health care and education. The decision-making process is inclusive, drawing on the diverse cultural, economic, and social perspectives across the continent to form policies that benefit the entire population. The administrative capital of Africa, potentially rotating among the major cities, serves as a hub for political and economic coordination. Regional economic zones specialize in industries based on regional strengths and resources and create a network of economic hubs that enhance continental economic integration. On the world stage, Africa speaks with one voice, as a major player in international politics. Its unified diplomatic voice commands respect and influence, shaping global policy on climate change, trade, and international security. Africa's role in global markets is transformative. With a unified regulatory environment and a vast common market, it attracts foreign direct investment on favorable terms. As such, it becomes a manufacturing and technology powerhouse.

Economic growth is dynamic and inclusive. The continent harnesses its vast natural resources responsibly and sustainably, transitioning from raw material exports to high-value processed goods and services. Renewable energy projects across the Sahara and along the coasts power the continent and become a significant export to global markets. Manufacturing businesses leverage Africa's rich natural resources to create value-added products. Instead of exporting raw materials, African businesses process minerals, agricultural products, and other resources locally, enhancing industrial output and reducing the reliance on foreign imports. This retains more wealth and creates millions of jobs.

Africa shifts from being seen as a market primarily for raw materials to a respected equal in international trade, offering high-quality, competitively priced goods and services. Trade agreements are renegotiated on terms that are favorable to African interests, respecting the continent's strategic goals of sustainable and equitable growth. The financial sector grows and provides the necessary services to support businesses and individuals. Institutions facilitate investment "pool" and provide capital for start-ups and large enterprises alike, further driving the continent's economic independence.

Start-ups, particularly in the tech sector, emerge as crucial players in Africa's economic landscape. These companies innovate solutions tailored to African needs, such as mobile banking, digital education platforms, health care apps, and agricultural tech that improves yield and sustainability. Innovation hubs such as those in Nairobi (Silicon Savannah) and Lagos expand across the continent, supported by government policies that encourage venture capital and innovation. Technology businesses thrive by creating products that are not only relevant to Africa but also globally competitive. These businesses leverage local talent and insights to build software and hardware solutions, fostering a digital economy that significantly reduces unemployment and opens new markets.

Open borders and a unified monetary policy boost intra-African trade, reducing dependency on external markets. This increases resilience against global economic shocks and creates a large, integrated market that attracts investment. A standardized education system ensures all Africa's children have access to quality education, creating a skilled workforce ready to tackle the continent's challenges. A unified health care system guarantees that all citizens have access to quality health care, improving overall life expectancy and quality of life. Collective investment in technology and infrastructure propels the continent forward. Innovations in agriculture, manufacturing, and services drive economic growth, with technology hubs similar to those in Nairobi and Lagos emerging across the continent.

Social support systems in this united Africa are robust, funded by a continent-wide welfare system that ensures no state is left behind. Social programs are tailored to the needs of diverse populations but maintain a standard that guarantees a minimum quality of life. In this new Africa, the continent significantly reduces its reliance on foreign investment by leveraging its own resources. The unified monetary policy and integrated economic strategies enable better capital mobilization within the continent. Revenues generated from local industries are reinvested into further developing the continental infrastructure and social programs.

In a unified Africa, the role of large businesses and start-ups is transformative, driving innovation, sustainability, and economic independence. By capitalizing on a single continental market and leveraging local resources and talents, Africa moves away from dependency on foreign investment. Instead, it builds an economy that is robust, diverse, and driven by the creativity and ingenuity of its people. This new economic paradigm not only propels Africa to new heights of prosperity but also redefines its position in the world as a powerhouse of economic and cultural significance.

Africa's leaders have honored their social contract, reduced corruption, and built trust from the ground up. This commitment has fostered trust between the government and its citizens, resulting in political stability and growth. With trust restored, investments have surged, and public services, including health care, education, and infrastructure, have improved significantly. Communities actively participate in governance, enhancing quality of life for all.

Shifting Gears Requires a Mindset Shift

I believe it is possible, and while there are myriad reasons Africa is underdeveloped today, it is possible to realize this vision, or any other vision of development, of success, of prosperity, of growth. Yet, I believe a shift is required if anything like this is to come to pass if anything truly ambitious is to come to fruition. And that's not because I think Africans don't want to achieve something like this, don't want to achieve growth or prosperity, don't want to thrive. No, it's because I think there are aspects to the African mindset that are self-limiting. And there may be many reasons for self-limiting mindset: history, cultural norms, apathy, a simple lack of ambition, a lack of inspiration perhaps. I believe that at the individual level people in Africa are extremely ambitious. So what's wrong? Why can't they realize their ambition?

At the corporate level, I see businesses of all types grappling with all sorts of challenges, and I work with many leaders to understand problems and understand the art of the possible so as to develop strategy and implement change. And at a corporate level, I see ambition, desire, and a need for growth that, too, is often not quite realized, especially when African companies are working with larger, foreign investors. In the corporate world, though, globally we are starting to develop a good understanding of leadership. We see that by empowering teams bottom up, you not only engender autonomous independent and efficient teamwork, but you create the leaders of tomorrow. The corporate world is grappling with tech-centric terms like "lean" and "agile" and is expected to be able to "move quick and break things" (like start-ups). So the corporate world has a different mindset from the start-up world. Businesses naturally have different mindsets from individuals. And government has a different mindset all together.

I think it comes down to ambition and leadership. And while I think we all, whether we are individuals or working for a company or a government, have ambition and leadership potential, we will act differently depending on our situation. This is a challenge; for if we want a unified Africa, we need individuals, businesses, and governments to unite under a shared vision and work together.

Introduction

IN THE BEGINNING, THERE WAS DIVISION

Anything, good or bad, is indeed possible, that is, if one has the will. It is absolutely possible to unite, and it's most definitely possible to divide. The problem we have in Africa, as we'll explore throughout this book, is not that we don't want to unite but that for generations we've been divided. These divisions have led to mistrust. In order to unite I believe we need to face these two very important and symbiotic issues: division and distrust. The first is, as most would expect, not the fault of Africans. We were divided long ago by others furthering their self-interest without care for the African people. Related to this, I think there's a persistent and troubling pattern of mistrust, competition, and envy that hinders our collective progress. In this chapter I examine both of these issues.

I am all about the future, all for looking and moving forward, but we need to briefly become historians if we are to understand how decisions made as far away as Berlin would dictate Africa's future for centuries and entrench divisions that still affect the continent today.

A CONFERENCE WITHOUT AFRICANS

The history of Africa's struggle for unity began with an event to which Africans had no seat at the table: the Berlin Conference of 1884–1885. This pivotal moment marked the beginning of modern Africa's fragmentation, not by the will of its people but by the strategic interests of European powers.

In the winter of 1884, fourteen nations gathered in Berlin, Germany, at the invitation of German Chancellor Otto von Bismarck. The conference was intended to regulate European colonization and trade in Africa, but it became the catalyst for what would later be known as the "Scramble for Africa"—the partitioning of an entire continent among European empires.

The attendees included Germany as the host, led by Bismarck, with Great Britain, France, Portugal (which already had control of the most territory), and then Belgium, Spain, Italy, the Netherlands, Austria-Hungary, Russia, Denmark, Sweden-Norway, the Ottoman Empire, and the United States, albeit with a minimal role. It was conspicuously absent of any African representatives. Not a single African leader, ruler, or community was consulted in the process that would determine their fate. Indeed, Africa's future was decided in rooms filled with men who had never set foot on much of the land they were claiming.

Figure 1. Gartenlaube 1884.[1]

[1] https://en.wikipedia.org/wiki/Berlin_Conference#/media/File:Afrikakonferenz.jpg

Dividing the Continent

The European powers agreed on a set of rules that would govern their colonization efforts. These included the following:

- Formalizing the partition of Africa: Each European power could claim land in Africa by notifying the others and demonstrating effective control. Borders were drawn with absolutely no regard for the ethnic, linguistic, or cultural realities of Africa.
- Guaranteeing free trade on African rivers: The Congo River and Niger River were opened to free trade, which mainly benefited European powers, not Africans.
- Recognizing the Congo free state: Belgium's King Leopold II was given personal control over the Congo, leading to one of the most brutal and exploitative regimes in colonial history.
- Pledging to end the slave trade: While the European nations pledged to eliminate the Arab and transatlantic slave trade, many turned to forced labor and other forms of exploitation instead. Slavery was abolished in name only.

In 1880, 10 percent of Africa was under European control. Over the next two decades, Africa was nearly entirely divided, with 90 percent of the continent falling under European rule by 1900.

The Legacy of Division

The consequences were devastating. New borders ignored existing African nations, tribes, and cultures, forcing rival ethnic groups to live together while splitting unified communities apart. This led to generations of ethnic and territorial conflicts, many of which persist today in civil wars, insurgencies, and border disputes.

African leaders were either replaced with European governors or reduced to mere figureheads, unable to exert control over their lands. Colonization introduced economic structures designed to benefit Europe at Africa's expense. Raw materials were extracted and sent to Europe, while African industries were discouraged from developing. Forced labor and exploitative taxation enriched European powers while keeping African populations impoverished.

While Africa has made strides toward unity since the end of colonial rule, scars of the Berlin Conference remain. Imposed structures and artificial borders continue to influence politics, economics, and cultural identities.

The Mindset of Dependency

The division of Africa reinforced a colonial mindset that viewed Africa as inferior and dependent on European control. Over time, this mindset was internalized, shaping how African nations interacted with the world and with each other post-independence.

THEN THERE WAS MISTRUST

I wanted to look at two reasons Africa is divided. The Berlin Conference is the first. It is a fact that this outrageous abuse of power by European leaders led to the divided continent we have today; as such, it's easy for us to acknowledge, and lay blame. The second reason, however, is perhaps harder for us to acknowledge or to swallow. It is not something that long-dead European leaders did to us; there is no other party to blame. In this instance, we need to look to ourselves.

I'm talking about the fact that Africans are distrustful of each other, to the point of sabotage. Throughout my life I've seen the subtle ways in which Africans, both on the continent and in the diaspora, tend to undermine each other. I find it deeply sad. It manifests in business, politics, education, and personal relationships. While external forces have played a role in cultivating this mindset, it is only we who can break the chain.

Mistrust among Africans: The Silent Saboteur

Mistrust among Africans, whether in Africa, the Caribbean, or among African Americans, has long been a barrier to unity. Instead of supporting and uplifting each other, there is often an underlying skepticism, a belief that another's success must come at one's expense. It leads to behaviors such as undermining, backbiting, and an unwillingness to collaborate, even when doing so would be mutually beneficial. I've seen it, and I've been a victim of it myself. In competitive team sports, I've seen teams generally support each other while those of African dissent have developed rivalries unmatched by others. In business, I've seen people resent Africans who progress in their roles or advance their careers. And personally, I've seen African Americans especially exhibit deep distrust of each other.

There's a phenomenon called "crab mentality," which describes how when one crab in a bucket tries to climb out the others pull it down, ensuring that no one escapes. I think this is reflected in African business ecosystems, in that successful entrepreneurs frequently find themselves isolated rather than celebrated. Instead of receiving support from peers, they face suspicion or even sabotage. African entrepreneurs, both in Africa and the diaspora, often struggle to gain support from their own communities. Unlike other ethnic groups that prioritize group economics, such as Chinese, Indian, Hispanic, and Jewish communities, Africans frequently distrust their own business leaders, opting instead to support foreign-owned enterprises.

In academic and professional settings, it's also prevalent. Rather than mentoring and supporting rising talents, senior professionals in many African institutions often withhold knowledge or opportunities out of fear that the younger generation may surpass them. African professionals in the US and Europe often express frustration that fellow Africans in leadership positions are more likely to block their growth rather than support them.

Another significant manifestation of mistrust is the strained relationship between African Americans and continental Africans. Despite sharing a common heritage, both groups often harbor negative perceptions of each other. African immigrants in the US sometimes view African Americans as entitled, while African Americans accuse African immigrants of being disconnected from racial struggles in America. Instead of working together to create economic and political influence, these groups often compete for resources and validation from non-Black communities.

As a natural collaborator, I share my thoughts, my work, and my ideas to help others, but also to gather valuable feedback. In doing so I have often lost friends and allies and seen my ideas taken as theirs. For me, it's fine; after all, ideas are cheap, as they say. But for Africans collectively I think it's holding us back.

The prevalence of mistrust among Africans stems from deep historical, psychological, and economic factors. Colonialism and slavery deliberately divided African communities, which of course fostered betrayal as a survival mechanism. The scarcity mindset, shaped by economic deprivation, reinforces competition over resources rather than collective growth. Internalized inferiority, instilled by decades of oppression, has led many Africans to trust outsiders over their own people. And then often the lack of institutional support leaves African communities without the strong economic and mentorship networks that other ethnic groups rely on for success.

There are many reasons for it. And to a great extent it is not our fault. But only we can make a change and break the cycle.

How do We Change This Self-Destructive Pattern?

I discuss mindset quite a bit in this book, but this is one example for which mindset really matters. As Africans, we must all shift from a scarcity mindset to an abundance mindset (on the way to a unified mindset, of course), recognizing that success is not a zero-sum game and that collective growth benefits everyone. Instead of tearing each other down, we should actively celebrate and support one another, buying from African businesses, mentoring young professionals, and promoting success stories.

Let's reframe competition as collaboration and drive mutual improvement rather than destruction. Let's ensure leaders open doors for others rather than gatekeep opportunities.

LET THERE BE UNITY

If Africa is to unite, the first step is recognizing the damage done by division and shifting the mindset from mistrust to collaboration and engagement. The continent cannot afford to be bound by borders that were never meant to serve its people. Africans must redefine unity on their own terms, through collaboration, economic empowerment, and strategic leadership.

The Berlin Conference was the beginning of division, but it does not have to define Africa's future. The mistrust that was built in our past doesn't have to define our future. The choice now is whether to continue to perpetuate division or to build a new model: designed for Africa, by Africa, with a vision for a truly united future.

SECTION 1

LET THERE BE UNITY

Chapter 1

DISRUPTING THE AFRICAN MINDSET

Did you know African nations are reticent to import food from other African nations, instead favoring to import food from elsewhere? "Before Russia's full-scale invasion of Ukraine in 2020, over 50 percent of fifteen African countries' imports of wheat came from Ukraine and Russia."[1]

You probably didn't know that, and honestly neither did I, until I started opening my eyes and ears to the data. In researching for this book, I have spoken to many people and explored many lines of inquiry, and everywhere I am faced with startling statistics. I'd say shock statistics—statistics that you read and think, "Surely they got that wrong," "But that makes no sense," "How can that be possible?" and "Why doesn't someone do something about that?"

IT DOESN'T ADD UP

Once I opened my eyes to see through the positive "initiatives" and "steps forward" and "strategic vision" and I looked at the data, two things happened. First, I experienced disbelief; then I felt anger. There are so many facts and figures that simply don't add up, it's hard to know where to start. Indeed, there could and probably should be many books just about these statistics.

Here though, I have pulled together the statistics I find the most shocking, those that add up the least, and those that clearly

[1] https://www.atlanticcouncil.org/blogs/econographics/ukraines-grain-exports-are-crucial-to-africas-food-security/

need tackling for Africa to move forward and for Africans to prosper:

- The continent accounts for roughly 65 percent of the world's diamond production. What if Africa was able to earn more from its diamonds by ensuring all its people benefitted more from this vast wealth?
- Africa is the youngest continent, with more than 60 percent of its population under the age of 25. This demographic trend presents both opportunities (e.g., a large workforce) and challenges (e.g., the need for jobs, education, and health care). What if Africa's leaders focused on youth empowerment and invested smartly to take advantage of a healthy, strong, and ambitious generation?
- Africa has around 30 percent of the earth's remaining mineral resources This includes over 40 percent of gold reserves and 90 percent of platinum reserves. What if it were able to strategically leverage this to achieve better terms with lenders, including foreign investment and the International Monetary Fund (IMF)?
- More than 70 percent of the world's cobalt is produced in the Democratic Republic of the Congo (DRC). What if the DRC halted cobalt production? Would the average consumers be able to afford Apple and other cell phone (mobile phones) devices?
- Africa is home to approximately 20 percent of the world's tropical forests, especially in Central and West Africa. The Congo Basin is the world's second-largest rainforest. These forests are vital for biodiversity and carbon storage and are sources of timber, though deforestation is a growing concern. What would the impact be on the planet if Africa is forced into further deforestation?
- Africa has an estimated 60 percent of the world's unused arable land. What if Africa made use of this land and became a center for global agricultural production?
- Ghana and Ivory Coast account for more than 60 percent of the world's cocoa production. What would be the impact of the Swiss economy and the price of chocolate if 60 percent of the world's cocoa production is stopped?

DISRUPTING THE AFRICAN MINDSET: FROM DIVIDED TO UNITED

In a world where rapid technological advancements and global connectivity reshape how we think about societal development, Africa stands at a pivotal juncture. The African continent, although rich in diversity and brimming with potential, faces unique historical, cultural, and socioeconomic challenges. These challenges are compounded by a prevailing mindset that often views Africa through the lens of its limitations rather than its vast possibilities. This book aims to challenge, disrupt, and change that mindset, moving from one that keeps Africa divided to one that unites it.

As a business leader with a deep history in helping some of the world's leading organizations innovate and evolve, I have witnessed firsthand the power of mindset in catalyzing change and fostering development. My journey, from advising major global corporations to navigating the complexities of various organizational cultures across continents, has equipped me with a unique set of skills and perspectives. Now, I aim to apply these problem-solving skills in a different context: helping the people of Africa, my homeland, to realize their potential.

Why focus on Africa? The question is not just of personal interest but of global significance. Africa is not simply a land of resources to be tapped; it is a vibrant continent with the potential to shape the global economic and cultural landscape over the coming decades. Yet, the potential of its greatest asset—its people—remains largely untapped due to persistent barriers in education, infrastructure, and, fundamentally, mindset.

A United Mindset

The "mindset problem" in Africa can be typified by a complex interplay of historical dependency, external narratives, and internalized limitations on ambition and innovation. This mindset is not merely an African issue but a global narrative that has often shaped international policy, business investment, and educational approaches toward the continent. Changing this mindset involves dismantling stereotypes, enhancing self-sufficiency, and nurturing a culture of innovation and entrepreneurship.

As part of my exploration of this topic, I have had the privilege to meet with and interview African entrepreneurs and business and political leaders. My conversations with them delved into their visions for the future, their insights on what is holding Africa back, and the innovative strategies they are employing to remove these blockers. Hearing directly from those leading change on the ground provided me with invaluable context and real-world perspectives on the challenges and opportunities facing the continent. Their insights have shaped my ideas and encouraged me to continue to research, probe, and challenge the path forward for Africa.

As a business leader, I view the transformation of Africa not through the simplistic lens of aid or intervention but through empowerment and partnership. This book proposes the shift from a mindset of dependency to one of empowerment, from a perceived incapacity to a celebration of capability. It is about recognizing the intrinsic value and potential of Africa's people and crafting strategies that are not imposed but developed through collaborative efforts.

Throughout this book I will explore various dimensions of the "mindset shift" required to unleash Africa's potential. I will delve into case studies, draw parallels with global success stories, and propose practical, scalable solutions that align with the continent's unique cultural and economic landscapes. The goal is to inspire a new narrative for Africa, one in which the continent is not merely emerging but is a vibrant leader in its own right.

Like others, I propose grand, complex, and expensive changes to help Africa fully grasp the opportunity. Unlike others, I also propose small-scale change that we can deliver today. I don't want to wait generations before Africa is prosperous. I want all Africans to benefit now.

This journey is not just about changing Africa; it's about changing how the world interacts with, and views Africa. It's about preparing a generation to take bold steps, equipped with knowledge, technology, and a vision for a prosperous future. Together, we can forge pathways that lead not only to economic growth but to a thriving society in which every individual can contribute to and benefit from a richer, more inclusive future.

As we embark on this journey, I invite you to rethink, reimagine, and reengage with what is possible for Africa and its people. Together, let's build a future that reflects and respects the true wealth of this dynamic continent: its people!

2063 Agenda

In 2013 the African Union published Agenda 2063 "The Africa We Want":

> AGENDA 2063 is Africa's blueprint and master plan for transforming Africa into the global powerhouse of the future. It is the continent's strategic framework that aims to deliver on its goal for inclusive and sustainable development and is a concrete manifestation of the Pan-African drive for unity, self-determination, freedom, progress, and collective prosperity pursued under Pan-Africanism and African Renaissance. The genesis of Agenda 2063 was the realization by African leaders that there was a need to refocus and reprioritize Africa's agenda from the struggle against apartheid and the attainment of political independence for the continent which had been the focus of The Organization of African Unity (OAU), the precursor of the African Union; and instead to prioritize inclusive social and economic development, continental and regional integration, democratic governance and peace and security amongst other issues aimed at repositioning Africa to becoming a dominant player in the global arena.[2]

Ultimately, Agenda 2063 is a set of aspirations, flagship programs, and a ten-year development plan that takes Africa toward

---

2 https://au.int/en

a more unified continent over a fifty-year time frame. Its aspirations are as follows:

1. A prosperous Africa based on inclusive growth and sustainable development
2. An integrated continent, politically united and based on the ideals of Pan-Africanism and the vision of Africa's Renaissance
3. An Africa of good governance, democracy, respect for human rights, justice, and the rule of law
4. A peaceful and secure Africa
5. An Africa with a strong cultural identity, common heritage, and shared values and ethics
6. An Africa whose development is people driven, relying on the potential of African people, especially its women and youth, and caring for children.
7. Africa as a strong, united, resilient, and influential global player and partner

The AU specified fifteen flagship projects to help deliver its aspirations:

1. Integrated High Speed Train Network
2. Formulation of an African Commodities Strategy
3. Establishment of the African Continental Free Trade Area (AfCFTA)
4. The African Passport and Free Movement of People
5. Silencing the Guns by 2020
6. Implementation of the Grand Inga Dam Project
7. Establishment of a Single African Air-Transport Market (SAATM)
8. Establishment of an Annual African Economic Forum
9. Establishment of the African Financial Institutions
10. The Pan-African e-Network
11. Africa Outer Space Strategy
12. An African Virtual and e-University
13. Cybersecurity
14. Great African Museum
15. Encyclopaedia Africana

It sounds pretty good, right? Who wouldn't want all these things for Africa? Indeed, these aspirations align with my own, and many of my ideas echo some of the flagship projects. Of course, developing Africa through unifying African nations is a good idea. No one can argue that these aren't well-intended aspirations or sound practical ideas for bringing those aspirations about. Yet critics of the Africa Agenda 2063 have raised several concerns.

Most criticism centers around ambition; the goals are seen by some to be too ambitious and, as such, unachievable. Without a clear definition of resource allocation and funding, the aspirations are deemed too hard for many African countries to commit to or fully realize. Furthermore, the lack of a concrete implementation plan means that the agenda is more of a statement of aspiration than a roadmap or blueprint. Indeed, the ten-year plans are just that: ten-year plans. And many of the deliverables from the first ten-year plan have already slipped. ("Silencing the Guns by 2020" has not been achieved.)

The agenda is believed by some to not properly address deep-rooted socioeconomic inequalities within and between African countries and, as such, it cannot be effective in lifting the poorest out of poverty. While I can sympathize with most of these viewpoints, I have far graver concerns about Agenda 2063.

Let's look first at the date. Why 2063? It seems like a rather arbitrary date to choose, a line in the sand, without much meaning. It is fifty years after the agenda was conceived in 2013, and roughly one hundred years since many African countries achieved independence, but other than allowing for a fifty-year implementation phase, the date really is meaningless.

"Planning fifty years ahead allows us to dream, think creatively, and sometimes crazy, to see us leapfrog beyond the immediate challenge," said African ministers during the 2014 Bahir Dar Ministerial Retreat on Agenda 2063.[3]

Indeed, a date so far in the future allows for a very long project timeline. You can, in fact you should, be ambitious. Some

[3] https://www.globalpartnership.org/blog/key-issues-agenda-2063-and-their-relevance-education-sector-africa

critics have argued that the goals set by Agenda 2063 are overly ambitious and may not be achievable within the given time frame. However, I would argue that the goals are not ambitious enough.

The agenda sets out what seems like some very ambitious goals. "World Class Infrastructure crisscrosses Africa" is a goal within aspiration 2: An integrated continent, politically united and based on the ideals of Pan-Africanism and the vision of Africa's Renaissance. "A Stable and Peaceful Africa" is also a goal within aspiration 4: A peaceful and secure Africa. These are not easy things to bring about quickly. But fifty years is surely too long to wait. People need help now. Why would we wait fifty years for these ideas to be realized?

"Healthy and well-nourished citizens" is a goal within aspiration 1: A prosperous Africa based on inclusive growth and sustainable development. Surely, we need this today. Similarly, "Full gender equality in all spheres of life" is a goal within aspiration 6: An Africa whose development is people driven, relying on the potential of African people, especially its women and youth, and caring for children. There's no viable reason to wait fifty years to accomplish these objectives.

Another issue I have with Agenda 2063 is that progress is unclear. Change needs to start immediately; otherwise, it won't happen. Perhaps there are initiatives currently in play, yet I don't see enough transparent tracking or measurement of these initiatives. From a simple management perspective, there's either not enough measurement or not enough transparency. This could be for a number of reasons: Perhaps the plan isn't clear or is still being developed; perhaps the reporting measures aren't in place, although there might be plenty of work underway behind the scenes; or perhaps nothing's happening, and no one's accountable. Perhaps various governments simply haven't really signed up to the plan. Perhaps, going back to my earlier point, this is really just an aspiration of a few well-intended people without the backing of enough of the leaders that matter. If the agenda were serious, it should come with a measurable plan so that all parties can track progress and risks, just like any good project.

In the corporate world, you would never expect a complex, multi-stakeholder, multiyear project to be delivered on time, or delivered at all, without a firm plan, success metrics, and progress reporting measures in place. It's hard enough delivering projects when they do have these things, let alone when they don't. Without firm plans, the fifty-year goal seems arbitrary. Why should it neatly take fifty years to implement?

I wonder if the fifty-year target is strategic in itself. Does distance give its authors a get-out clause? The politicians in government today, and when the agenda was envisioned, are unlikely to be in government in fifty years' time. Indeed, we should hope that they are not. If you know you're not going to be in power at the goal date, you can worry less about whether that goal is achieved. Most political cycles run for four years, with most politicians not wanting to commit to ambitions or pledges in their own session, let alone fifty years into the future. Putting the target so far ahead allows you to distance yourself from any non-delivery. It also allows you to blame those that came after you. You get to say, "It was them, not me, who failed to deliver."

Creating a vision that is so far out looks to me to be political for other reasons. Why? Well because you don't have to upset any incumbents if your plans for radical change will only come after their lifetime. Imagine you are promoting a radical shake-up in how governments are run. You want to end corruption, make government transparent, and give the people much more of a voice. This might sound like too much of a radical shake-up to many leaders and abhorrent to those who benefit from corrupt practices. But if you tell them it's only happening in fifty years, they'll feel much more comfortable about it. You give them plenty of time to carry on operating as they operate today, amassing their personal fortunes at the expense of their electorate. Not only do you give them time to continue acting with impunity, but any real change will only come in when they've retired, are in old age, or after they're dead! As such, your vision will get passed by all leaders, as it really doesn't impact them at all and requires no real change from them. They can leave much if not all of it to those that come after them, all while signaling what a great idea it is.

The agenda also relies on continual support from the IMF, and, as I discuss later, the IMF imposes significant conditions on borrowing countries that devalue local currencies, keeping people in poverty. Any agenda whose remit is to require substantial further funding from the IMF needs to be sanity checked. While Africa may need the infrastructure the agenda proposes, how it is funded needs careful consideration. Any vision that is simply about a continued reliance on IMF funding is, to me, a problem for Africa, and not a plan for sustainable development. Indeed, the agenda relies on many external funding sources, including foreign investment, aid, and international cooperation. I believe that greater emphasis should be placed on building internal capacities and self-sufficiency. If Africa can instead focus on diversifying its industries and building self-sufficiency, it will need less reliance on external funding.

The increasing threat of neocolonialism is a problem, not least because many in Africa don't see it. I believe true independence is only achieved when African nations are able to sustain their own economies. The agenda cannot rely on foreign investment that comes with so many strings attached that it binds Africa to new colonial powers, including but not limited to Russia and China.

Responsibility is a key issue for me. If you want to set up a fifty-year long project, you have to think carefully about who is going to deliver it, understand that all those involved are project stakeholders, and engage and manage those stakeholders appropriately. The agenda puts the onus on governments to deliver, but what it fails to acknowledge is that it is the youth of today, indeed some who are not even born yet, who will deliver this plan for future generations. To make such a long plan a success, clear attention must be paid to how to harness the generations coming through to not only deliver, but to build on the vision you have today.

Some critics highlight the need for greater public awareness and participation in the agenda. They argue that for Agenda 2063 to be successful it needs to be embraced by the African people, and there should be mechanisms in place to ensure their involvement in the planning and implementation processes. While the agenda was created after having consulted African citizens, the current plans do not contain many mechanisms for public engagement.

While Agenda 2063 contains good ideas and nice-to-haves, I don't believe it will come to pass unless you first change the African mindset. You can say "this is the Africa we want" all you want, but an Africa rife with conflict and corruption simply can't deliver on the promises set out here.

So, what's the alternative? Limit the scale and duration of the ambition? Only ever publish simpler, nearer-term aspirations? Get busy with project costing and planning for every element? Engage with more citizens to win support? Or go bigger or faster or more radical?

Well, my alternative vision starts with mindset instead of with infrastructure project deliverables. I believe that it is possible to achieve effective development, but first you need to affect great change, not in what you do or what you have but in how you think.

Oh, and then I believe you have to start small.

WHAT IF?

Framing big challenges as "what ifs" is a model I favor for exploring the complex challenges facing Africa today. This approach not only opens up a space for imaginative thinking but also sidesteps the constraints of current realities, allowing us to envision the possibilities of transformative change.

The what if model serves as a powerful tool to provoke thought, inspire innovation, and challenge the status quo. By asking "What if?" I invite readers to consider alternative realities and the potential impacts of making bold decisions or adopting new perspectives. I hope to break down complex issues into understandable, relatable, and discussable elements.

In my last book, *A Better Vision for the Future of Work*, I used what-if scenarios to explore futuristic workplaces, the evolution of leadership styles, and the integration of technology in daily work life. These scenarios were not just speculative; they were backed by strategic insights and real-world implications, encouraging readers to think critically about the paths we choose today and their long-term effects on our collective future.

Here, I continue to use the what-if format to delve into key topics affecting Africa. It is important to note that I do not pretend to have all the answers. As I ponder these questions and challenges, most open up yet more new challenges and pose an increasing number of unanswered questions. And it is okay, and has to be okay, to have unanswered, indeed unanswerable questions. Changing Africa is possible, but changing Africa is complex; many things need to change.

By imagining different futures through these what-if scenarios, I aim to spark a broader dialogue among stakeholders, policymakers, business leaders, and the people, especially the youth of Africa. The ultimate goal is to foster a proactive approach to opening debate and discussion, as it is only then that can we craft innovative and inclusive solutions, paving the way for a prosperous and unified continent.

The what if model challenges us all to think bigger (and smaller) and bolder and more courageously about the future we wish to create for Africa.

Chapter 2

WHAT'S MINDSET GOT TO DO WITH IT?

We've looked at an imagined future, one full of prosperity, and shortly we'll look at lessons from elsewhere. But what's missing? And could something as simple as mindset have something to do with it?

Transformation and development are not all about investment and infrastructure. It's not all about defining and moving toward a vision. First, before you can even define and agree on a vision, before you even dream to imagine, you need to have the right mindset.

You may well ask, "What does mindset have to do with African development? Does it have anything at all to do with it?" Well, I think it absolutely does.

Mindset can be the difference between thinking big and thinking small, the difference between negotiating hard and getting a poor deal, and the difference between thinking you'll never get out of debt and grasping every opportunity.

WHAT DO WE MEAN BY MINDSET?

I'd like to clarify what I mean by mindset, as, quite rationally, your understanding of mindset may differ from mine. Many people talk about mindset, and we often assume we have a shared understanding of the concept, but I want to explore this in a bit.

"Mindset" refers to the underlying beliefs and attitudes that shape how we perceive and respond to various situations, challenges, and opportunities in life. It influences the way we think, feel, and behave. Mindset is closely linked to our approach to learning, effort, and personal development. Our mindset influences how we approach pretty much anything.

There is even such a thing as mindset theory, developed by psychologist Carol Dweck.[4] Dweck's definition revolves around the concepts of fixed and growth mindsets. Individuals with a fixed mindset believe their abilities, intelligence, and talents are static traits that cannot be significantly developed. If you believe your intelligence and traits are fixed, you may desire to appear smart and may try to avoid challenges. You may not try very hard, and you may give up easily. People with a growth mindset, on the other hand, believe their abilities and intelligence can be developed by working at things and putting in the effort. They have a love for learning, resilience in the face of setbacks, and a greater willingness to embrace challenges and learn from criticism.

Mindset is not just a term used to describe our ability to learn new things; it is universally understood to describe how we respond to all sorts of things. Do you have a positive mindset? Or a negative one? Do you have a scarcity mindset or an abundance mindset? Do you have a success mindset? Mindset simply means your approach to things. But it goes a little deeper because mindset is not necessarily something you consciously control.

I believe our mindsets are hardwired and shaped by a lifetime's worth of conditioning and external influence: what we've learned, who we know, where we go, and what we experience. These things affect how we approach things subconsciously, before we are able to make logical reasoned judgments.

WHAT'S YOUR MINDSET?

Do you think you have a fixed or a growth mindset? I think we'd all like to imagine we have a growth mindset. A growth mindset

[4] https://profiles.stanford.edu/carol-dweck

according to Dweck seems like a positive; why be of a fixed mindset when you can achieve anything with a growth mindset?

Do you have a divided mindset or a united one? The terms "divided mindset" and "united mindset" are not necessarily terms you'll have heard already. They're terms I will explore and explain in this chapter. For now though, how do these terms make you feel, and do you feel you have a natural affinity with one or the other?

SHIFTING YOUR MINDSET

So, can your mindset change? While I think mindset is shaped through the sum total of our experiences, I believe you can change your mindset, for example from a fixed mindset to a growth mindset or from a scarcity mindset to an abundance mindset. You can develop a success mindset. Furthermore, on a personal level, there are all sorts of people and services out there who'd like to help you change your mindset, to get you thinking "right." Mindset shift is an industry in itself.

Mindset coaching has seen significant growth recently, driven by a cultural shift toward self-improvement and personal development. Helping individuals cultivate a more positive or growth-oriented mindset is promoted as helping people achieve better outcomes in all sorts of areas of life, from career to relationships, to well-being. The appeal lies in the promise of transformation through mental and emotional shifts, the implication being if you can change things yourself, you don't need to rely on external changes or other people and situations. You have the power. There are plenty of people chasing self-improvement through one sort of mindset shift or another.

UNDERSTANDING ORGANIZATIONAL MINDSET

Mindset need not be the domain of individuals only. Groups and organizations can have a collective mindset too. The term "organizational mindset" refers to the collective attitudes, beliefs, and values that shape how people within an organization perceive and respond to various things. It includes how an organization approaches challenges, opportunities, relationships, and change.

An organization's mindset influences its culture, decision-making processes, and overall effectiveness. If you work in a company or organization of any size, you will innately understand its mindset, at least if you've been there a while. To understand the mindset of an organization, we need to look at the organization's reaction to failure and success, how it attracts and nurtures its people, the way feedback is given and received, the wider communication style, the approach to innovation and risk taking, and its overall attitude toward growth and development. Mindset is not the same as culture, although the two are interlinked; to me, culture is what an organization feels like, whereas mindset is how an organization thinks.

For organizations, a fixed mindset would look like "This is how we do things here," whereas a growth mindset would be typified by a "How might we achieve something new?" attitude. An organizational mindset is not the same as the mindset of the individuals within the organization. Often, employees start to act in a way that is aligned with the organizational mindset rather than their own beliefs, whether they agree with the organizational mindset or not. Group think comes into play a lot, and culture keeps people all organizationally thinking the same.

CAN A COUNTRY OR A CONTINENT HAVE A MINDSET?

I think countries, too, can exhibit a mindset in their policies and cultural attitudes. For example, a country with a fixed mindset might resist change, cling to traditional ways of doing things, and be less open to new ideas or external influences. This could hinder progress and development. On the other hand, a country with a growth mindset embraces change, innovation, and the continuous development of its citizens' skills and knowledge. A growth mindset at the country level can lead to greater economic growth, social progress, and a more dynamic and competitive presence on the global stage.

And at the continental level, can there be a single mindset that unites billions of people and diverse countries? Possibly. Let's look at Europe. The European mindset could be typified by a strong sense of tradition and history, mixed with a progressive liberal outlook underpinned by social safety nets and social justice. Diplomacy and cooperation are prized. Individual rights and freedoms are highly valued. This is not a mindset in itself; rather, these things might instead be considered traits.

It's not to say that everyone in Europe agrees or exhibits all of these European traits; instead, at a continental level, Europe's interactions with the rest of the world are based on these principles. The shared traits mean that decisions about policy are guided by an often-unwritten set of guide rails as well as an explicitly written set of rules. I believe that all these traits together give rise to what I call a "united mindset."

At the time of writing this book, there is change taking place in European politics. It seems the European mindset is shifting. Collaboration and a desire to be governed by the European Union (the united mindset) is becoming less well favored. There is a rise in the popularity of hard right and far-right politicians and policies. The latest EU elections have seen a massive swing to the right and away from a more united mindset. There are many reasons for this: War in Ukraine has pushed the cost of living up even further after the end of the COVID-19 pandemic, Europeans feel poorer and less prosperous and want to take back control of their economies, and there are issues with borders and the electoral process.

In this book, I advocate for a united Africa. While the European love affair with centralized governance is fading, in part because it did not bring the prosperity it promised, I still believe that Africa is better united on many issues. First though, I want to explore the African mindset and whether there is an African mindset at all.

WHAT IS AFRICA'S MINDSET?

The concept of an "African mindset" is, of course, complex and diverse and reflects the vast array of cultures, histories, and social dynamics across the continent. While I want to approach the subject with sensitivity and an appreciation for the diversity of a continent of over 1.2 billion people, there are some characteristics stereotypically associated with Africans. These characteristics are, in my mind, overwhelmingly positive.

I believe stereotypes are stereotypes for a reason; there's no smoke without fire, so to speak. So, while not every African exhibits all of these character traits, I find these stereotypes rather appealing, and they make me proud to be African.

AFRICAN PEOPLE ARE COMMUNITY CENTRIC AND GENEROUS

One of the most unifying concepts across many African cultures is the philosophy of ubuntu, often summarized by the phrase "I am because we are." Ubuntu emphasizes compassion, respect, and deep bond among individuals. In many African societies, communal living and mutual aid are deeply ingrained practices, ensuring that people look out for one another, share resources, and collaborate. The communal mindset fosters resilience, cohesion, and belonging. African people simply tend to understand that they are connected, and they help each other.

AFRICAN PEOPLE ARE RESILIENT AND STRONG

Many Africans have a strong sense of resilience and adaptability due to a combination of factors. Historically, we have endured a lot so naturally have built our resilience through ancestral, familial, and personal experience. Religious and spiritual beliefs also contribute, provide hope, and give strength.

AFRICAN PEOPLE ARE RESPECTFUL AND PROUD

Among Africans, there is a deep respect for elders and traditions. Elders are often seen as custodians of wisdom and culture, and their guidance is highly valued. More than just respecting elders, however, Africans respect each other. Africans are also proud; we're proud of ourselves, our families and communities, and our nations. In my view, this pride comes from the strong foundation of respect.

AFRICAN PEOPLE ARE CREATIVE AND TENACIOUS

Many Africans demonstrate a remarkable ability to innovate and find creative solutions to problems. This is, in part, because they have been used to doing with less and have to make less stretch further. Creativity has been nurtured intergenerationally, passed down as a skill, which enables modern Africans to be incredibly entrepreneurial.

TRAITS VERSUS MINDSETS

There are so many positive traits here that can be harnessed to deliver many of the ideas set out in this book. These are the traits that make the people and the continent of Africa what it is. However, these are personality or character traits rather than mindsets. Traits and mindsets both play significant roles in shaping our behavior, personality, and the way we interact with the world, but there's a clear difference between the two concepts.

A trait is a stable characteristic or quality that we possess. Traits stay with us over time and are generally considered inherent. A mindset, on the other hand, is a way of thinking, an attitude, or a set of beliefs that influence how we interpret and respond to situations. Mindsets can be fluid and are shaped by experiences, education, and conscious reflection. Mindsets can change over time.

Furthermore, it is important to acknowledge that we can have multiple mindsets at any given time. We can have both a growth mindset and a collaboration mindset, for example.

SO, IS THERE AN AFRICAN MINDSET?

I don't think there is a specific "African mindset"—no one mindset typifies Africa. But there are mindsets that can be cultivated and harnessed, and there are mindsets that may need to be discouraged.

For example, we might all accept it is beneficial to have a growth mindset over a fixed mindset, and we can have a growth mindset regardless of our personality traits. We might be creative, tenacious, and proud, and also have a growth mindset. So no, there's no African mindset, but there are mindsets that I think Africans need to harness.

POSITIVE MINDSETS

Positive mindsets encourage growth, resilience, and overall well-being. I want to look at what some of these commonly understood positive mindsets might be and how applicable they are to sustainable development in Africa.

A growth mindset is the belief that abilities and intelligence can be developed through dedication and hard work. People with a growth mindset see challenges as opportunities to learn and improve rather than as threats. Clearly a growth mindset could be hugely beneficial to young people in Africa as they develop their careers in new, diversified industries, realizing a new role for themselves and contributing to a growing economy.

Resilience mindset involves the ability to bounce back from setbacks and adversity. It's characterized by perseverance, adaptability, and the ability to maintain a positive outlook even in difficult situations. Many in Africa naturally have a resilience mindset out of necessity. A resilience mindset may be seen as positive, but it shouldn't be necessary as it's born out of adversity.

An abundance mindset is the belief that there are enough resources and opportunities for everyone. People with an abundance mindset are more likely to share, collaborate, and celebrate others' successes rather than feeling threatened by them. An abundance mindset often requires somewhat of a leap of faith, especially if you are not someone surrounded by great riches. An abundance mindset can also be used hand in hand with prosperity theology to exploit people; for example, if you are told to contribute a great proportion of your own resources for the greater good on the promise it will be returned to you many times over.

An optimistic mindset is the tendency to focus on the positive aspects of situations and expect favorable outcomes. While it is a pleasant mindset, it doesn't factor in reality or risk and can result in people being taken advantage of.

A gratitude mindset involves recognizing and appreciating the good things in life. A gratitude mindset seems to me to be less relevant when dealing with real-world issues, which by their nature pose significant challenges.

A curiosity mindset is about being open to new experiences, ideas, and knowledge. An empathy mindset is the ability to understand and share the feelings of others. These are all positive, but in my mind not all that important when it comes to lifting people out of poverty.

UNITED MINDSET

I propose that a united mindset is what Africa needs to develop if it is to successfully end conflict and poverty, harness its resources, support its people, and take its true place on the world stage. A united mindset refers to a collective way of thinking that emphasizes unity, collaboration, and shared purpose. It is the opposite of a divided mindset, when fragmentation and discord are prevalent. A united mindset is driven by the belief that, together, people can achieve more than they can individually. This mindset fosters cooperation, mutual respect, and pursuit of common goals, leading to stronger communities, more effective teams, and greater societal progress.

People see themselves as part of a larger whole, working toward shared objectives. They prioritize collective well-being over individual gain and are motivated by the success of the community. They value cooperation and collaboration, believing that pooling resources, knowledge, and efforts leads to better outcomes than working in isolation or competition. This encourages teamwork, open communication, and a willingness to help others.

People think beyond immediate gains, focusing on sustainable outcomes that benefit future generations. They are more likely to prioritize long-term goals over short-term profits, ensuring the well-being of all over time.

A united mindset is inclusive, recognizing and valuing the contributions of all members. It fosters resilience, as individuals support each other through challenges and changes, and it fosters a sense of togetherness, as the focus is on what can be achieved collectively rather than individually.

NEGATIVE MINDSET

Of course, there are also negative mindsets that can hinder personal growth and create barriers to success. As I mentioned, a fixed mindset is the belief that abilities and intelligence are static and cannot be changed. It can limit personal growth and can prevent people from reaching their full potential. I do suspect, however, that a fixed mindset has become very unpopular as it is the antithesis of a growth mindset. Prior to the identification of a growth mindset, many more people were of this fixed mindset.

Other negative mindsets include victim mentality, which is the idea that you are always at the mercy of external forces and that you have little to no control over your life, and a scarcity mindset, which is the belief that there is not enough money, success, love, or other resources to go around.

DIVIDED MINDSET

What about a divided mindset? Is it even a thing? Well yes, I believe it is. A divided mindset is when a person or group perceives the world through the lens of separation, conflict, and competition rather than unity, collaboration, and common purpose. It is characterized by focusing on differences rather than similarities, which can lead to disunity, mistrust, and a lack of cohesion within teams, communities, or even entire nations. Sound familiar? I see a divided mindset at the core of many African conflicts and regional tensions. I see a divided mindset as responsible for a lack of cohesion, for conflict, and for slow development.

COLONIAL MINDSET

There might be something else going on, however. What if it is not just a divided mindset that is at fault? What if Africa has in some way a colonial mindset? How could the African mindset be colonial so many years after independence? The concept of a colonial mindset suggests that despite the formal end of colonialism, many African countries and people have internalized certain aspects of colonial ideologies that continue to shape ways of thinking, governance, and societies.

Some argue that a colonial mindset is one that maintains Western power and governance structures, or one that has a preference for foreign goods over local ones. Yet I see a colonial mindset in the continued reliance on former colonial powers for economic and political guidance and a lack of confidence in Africa's ability to solve its own problems. I do believe that remnants of a colonial mindset are what causes Africa to negotiate from a position of weakness. The colonial mindset is a double negative. It's perceived as bad to have a colonial mindset whichever way it plays out; who would want to be seen as thinking like a colonial power or still being influenced by the legacy of colonialism?

HOW DOES MINDSET CONTRIBUTE TO DEVELOPMENT?

Why does mindset matter so much, and how does it relate to development? In my mind, mindset plays a crucial role in development at the country level by influencing attitudes, behaviors, and policies that drive progress. A country's collective mindset can shape its approach to innovation, education, health, governance, defense, and international relations.

Let's look at innovation. One way mindset contributes to development is through fostering a culture of innovation and entrepreneurship; indeed, as is widely accepted, Africans are already highly entrepreneurial. At the country level, when a country adopts a growth mindset it encourages its citizens to take risks, experiment with new ideas, and pursue new ventures. This can lead to the creation of new businesses and the development of new technologies. Countries with a supportive environment for innovation often see higher rates of economic growth and job creation.

Education is another critical area in which mindset impacts development. A collective mindset that values education and lifelong learning promotes investment in quality education systems and access to educational opportunities for all citizens. This, in turn, builds a skilled and knowledgeable workforce capable of driving economic growth and addressing complex challenges.

In governance, mindset influences the effectiveness and integrity of institutions. A mindset that emphasizes transparency, accountability, and public service can lead to more effective governance and the implementation of policies that promote social and economic development. Conversely, a mindset that tolerates corruption and inefficiency can hinder progress and undermine public trust in government institutions.

The collective mindset also affects social cohesion and the ability to address social issues. A united mindset that values inclusivity, equality, and social justice can foster a more harmonious and cooperative society. This can lead to policies that reduce inequality, protect human rights, and ensure that all citizens have the opportunity to contribute to and benefit from economic development.

Internationally, mindset shapes a country's approach to global cooperation and trade. A mindset that embraces globalization and international collaboration can lead to the formation of beneficial trade partnerships, participation in international organizations, and the adoption of best practices from around the world.

Mindset also influences how a country addresses challenges such as environmental sustainability. A forward-thinking mindset that recognizes the importance of environmental conservation and sustainable development can lead to policies that protect natural resources, reduce carbon emissions, and promote renewable energy.

Africa will need a mindset that includes the traits of risk taking, accountability, collaboration, global approach, a full belief in education and development, and a willingness to forgo near-term gains for future prosperity. Africa needs a united mindset.

PROBLEMS WITH THE AFRICAN MINDSET

Are there problems with the current perceived African mindset? Am I blaming the people for their current situation of being marred in debt to the world's richest nations? Am I blaming how people think? No, I am not blaming Africans. Or Africa. But when you want to make a change, you have to understand where you're coming from and where you're going. You have to assess the current state, and you have to undertake a gap analysis. When you keep doing the same thing over and over again, you tend to keep getting the same result. If you suffer under colonial rule, you're equally as likely to suffer under the control of the International Monetary Fund (IMF) or indebtedness to China or Russia, or to Meta or Alphabet, for that matter. Ridding yourself of colonial powers only to be indebted again under a subtler but ever more pervasive neocolonialism is simply no good.

So how does Africa end up in debt to richer powers time and time again? Is mindset to blame? I believe Africa comes to negotiations from a position of lack, and in doing so it gets a perpetually bad deal from whomever it is negotiating with. Africa's leaders sell Africa short by failing to properly value their hand. Could a change in mindset help leaders negotiate better?

You can have generosity, strength, resilience, and pride as much as you like, but unless you can stand up to a richer negotiator with a deep understanding of your future wealth and future value, you can't negotiate for yourself well. To come out with a better deal, a deal that sets Africa up for prosperity, leaders have to be able to negotiate from a much stronger position.

Put simply, the problem with the African mindset is that it is divided. It is not powerful; it is weak. It cannot excel; it is held back. It does not seek to make its own way; it looks to others for support.

At the core of the problem is its individualistic approach. The fact that countries are divided, that Africa is divided, compounds the problem. Each country comes from a position of relative weakness compared to the might of those with whom they negotiate. When a country negotiates a deal from a position of weakness it will accept poorer terms than if it negotiates from a position of strength. To negotiate from a position of strength, a country needs a united mindset.

Imagine what your mindset would be if you knew Africa was one nation. Imagine the strength with which you negotiate trade deals, negotiate investments, negotiate loans, and negotiate global politics. You are able to draw on all your collective strengths, all your collective power. This strength becomes entrenched in all that you do; it shapes your mindset and your approach to everything. At a country level, unification can enable a shift in mindset and open up a world of opportunity.

At a corporate level, organizations large and small can compete on a more equal footing if Africa is united and their mindset is united. Your business being based in one African country puts you at a disadvantage, whereas if you are an African business, based in a united Africa, your mindset naturally understands the realm of opportunity is automatically continental—your scope for growth is manifold that of a company in a divided Africa. The mindset of a united Africa allows continental corporations and start-ups alike to compete on a global scale.

And on a personal, individual level, imagine having the weight of debt and poverty lifted from your shoulders. Imagine knowing you were part of a united continent, and your continent offered opportunity equal to what you might find elsewhere. As a citizen of a united continent, you're able to develop your skills and your career as you wish, grasping opportunities near home or farther away. You can develop wealth and support your family, now and in the future. You enjoy a sense of stability and potential. Instead of worrying about instability, insurgency, and conflict near home, you are able to plan and grow. The mindset shift you experience personally spurs you on to grasp the opportunities available to you; it stops you worrying about future debt, currency fluctuations, or inflation; it helps you take your place in a diverse and equitable continental society. How does this new united mindset feel on a personal level? In addition to all the African traits of being creative and tenacious, generous and community spirited, resilient and strong, respectful and proud, a united mindset also engenders a sense of positivity, certainty, and belief.

Other cultures are so full of self-belief and certainty in their ability to achieve they are criticized as being entitled. "Entitlement" is often a dirty word. I don't suggest anyone should feel entitled to wealth without earning it, but shouldn't people everywhere feel entitled to opportunity? Wouldn't it be good if Africans felt entitled to fair opportunity to develop their skills and contribute to a burgeoning economy? Wouldn't it be a good thing if Africans grew up feeling a clear sense of entitlement to good health, to education, to living free from conflict in a society free from corruption in which they could develop their skills, earn well, and build wealth just like their counterparts elsewhere in the world can?

Instead of entitlement, with all its negative connotations, I prefer to look at this as empowerment. I desperately want all Africans to feel empowered—empowered to live their life on fair terms, unimpeded by debt negotiated from a position of weakness that indebts them to a never-ending cycle of unfair terms and holds them in poverty. I strongly believe a united Africa can facilitate a united mindset and that a united mindset empowers everyone.

CAN AFRICA CHANGE ITS MINDSET?

So, can we change mindset? Well, people, organizations, and governments can change pretty much anything if they have the will. The United Arab Emirates (UAE) creating a new country in a few short decades is testament to that.

As my background is in organizational transformation and change management, I want to look at what Africa can learn from change theory. I help organizations to change how they work and how they think, to change their products and solutions and their mindset. I'm a firm believer in mindset on both a personal and organizational level, and I believe it is possible to understand and change both a personal and organizational mindset to achieve previously unimaginable goals. I also believe it is possible to change or develop the collective mindset of large groups of people but that this requires a different approach.

Changing an organizational mindset requires a deliberate approach; that's when change management comes in. The change process allows an organization to move from one state to another in a methodical way. As I've helped many organizations achieve change, I know it is possible to move from one state into a totally different one (i.e., to make big, sweeping changes, even in the face of significant opposition and resistance). The change management discipline is one that is well understood in an organizational context; it can almost be formulaic—easy, if you like.

USING CHANGE MANAGEMENT THEORY TO CHANGE THE MINDSET OF AN ORGANIZATION

Effective change management, mobilization, and readiness begin with strong, committed leadership. Leaders articulate a clear vision for the change, communicate its importance, and then support the process. Their commitment generally sets the tone for the rest of the organization and provides a model for behavior and attitudes. They lead the way.

Any successful change initiative in a corporate setting requires a clear and compelling vision that outlines the desired future state; it needs to state where you want to go. This vision is then communicated to all stakeholders. Transparent communication is essential and ensures everyone understands the reasons for the change, the benefits it will bring, and their role in the transition. Effective communication builds trust.

Involving stakeholders in the change process increases their commitment and reduces resistance. In an organization, involving employees through consultations, feedback sessions, and collaborative planning fosters a sense of ownership and empowerment. Resistance to change is entirely normal and is found in any change process. There will always be people and groups who don't understand, disagree with, or oppose the change. Some will even seek to stop it. A good leader's job is to identify sources of resistance and address them through empathy, support, and clear communication. Leaders need to mitigate concerns and help people come to terms with and accept the future state as desirable. They have to "sell the vision."

Then practical training and support is delivered to equip people with the skills and knowledge they need to adapt. In a corporate setting, training programs and ongoing support help employees feel confident in their new roles. This phase could take significant time and resources, depending on the nature of the change.

Ensuring that the change is sustained over the long term requires embedding it into an organization's culture. All change is monitored and measured, and success metrics are communicated to all stakeholders.

You might think this is all a rather long-winded way of saying that any big change needs a clear vision, careful communication, and sensitive introduction and measurement and that all those people affected by the change should be considered and supported at all times. The point here, though, is that no change is possible when it is not properly managed. No change simply just happens accidentally, in organizations or anywhere else for that matter. The change process in the corporate world is there to enable change, to make sure change happens as desired. It is a discipline in itself, with specific roles, rules, and techniques.

If you want to effect change in an organization of any size, you consider change properly; you make a plan, and you may even bring in experts to help. And as one of those experts, with this model I've seen successful change that's big and small, from changing technical processes in a small enterprise to changing culture in a global organization. I know that what might seem to be difficult change is indeed possible. Ultimately, I believe that people can achieve what they set their minds to with the right conditions and the right leadership.

USING CHANGE MANAGEMENT THEORY TO CHANGE THE MINDSET OF A CONTINENT

What strikes me is that something so well understood in a business and commercial context has no real counterpart in the world of governance and politics. It is possible to define a culture and an ethos within an organization and expect that employees will follow suit in adopting a particular way of doing things. It is not possible to do this on a country level, though; politicians or civil servants cannot tell a population what or how to think or how to act. Governance is there to serve the people, not the other way around, so a top-down mindset change is not a plausible or desirable outcome. I am interested in how we can learn lessons from organizational structures at the country level and how we might define mindset shifts that can be supported to facilitate Africa's development.

I believe we need to shift the mindset of the political elite, corporations operating in Africa, *and* the African people. We need to shift the mindset from a divided one that accepts a poor deal too often to a stronger, united mindset that feels empowered to grasp opportunity.

I don't think this can be a top-down process, dictated by leaders to citizens. I think change needs to be instigated and led at every level. Instead of focusing on unification, which must be brought about at the political level, I want to focus on empowerment, which can and should happen at all levels. By empowering people, specifically young people, in Africa, we can shift their mindset from a young age, and we can help all Africans adopt the mindset of unity and of growth.

EMPOWERMENT: AT THE HEART OF THE NEW UNITED AFRICAN MINDSET

My idea is that by offering people and businesses new opportunities, and by empowering them to participate in politics and societal change, you instantly shift their mindset and enable them to achieve much more than they would otherwise. Let's look at how to shift mindset through empowerment.

There are three critical layers to consider: the mindset of the people, the mindset of corporations, and the mindset of political leaders. I believe that the many positive aspects of the African mindset need to be harnessed to empower Africa. To do this we need to invert the power structure. Bear with me for my explanation as to why.

I like to look at the African mindset through three layers or lenses: people, corporations, and political leaders. The African people have a strong mindset, the ability to grow, and the desire to succeed. African businesses similarly have strong optimism and entrepreneurship but feel they need some assistance. African leaders have large problems to solve, a desire to make a mark, but time and time again turn to the outside for support. At the same time, they see their population as needing to be served and their commercial sector as in need of inward investment. They have big issues to solve.

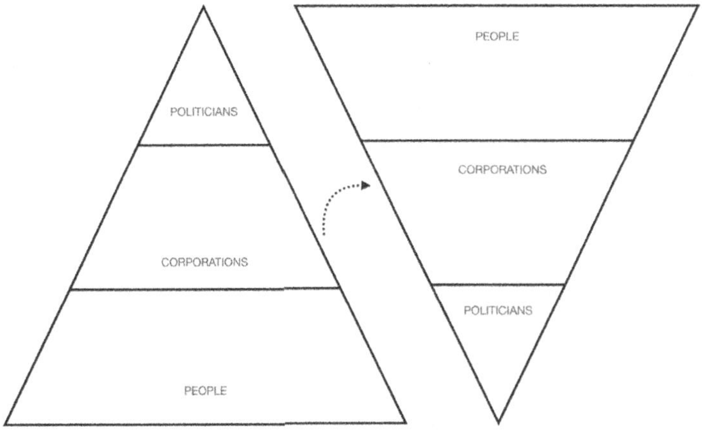

Figure 2. The shift in power.

I place the three groups in my diagram, with leaders at the top, corporations in the middle, and the people at the bottom. Decisions that affect everyone are taken by those at the top, the political leaders. The fate of the corporations operating in Africa, be they homegrown or multinational, is also determined by decisions made by political leaders. If politicians can't support enough Africans into the workforce or the middle class, businesses will not have enough customers for their products and services. Corporations need Africans to thrive. Yet the decisions made by corporations also affect both political leaders and the people. They affect the people because they set the price of goods and services (to an extent), and they determine where corporations wish to invest and in what. Corporations impact political leaders because they can bring significant investment and boost economies. The people have less influence. Sure, they can vote in most countries in a "democratic" process, but all too often they are not offered real choice, and leaders and parties often stay in power for many terms, keeping things the same for decades. At the top of the pyramid, the leaders have all the power, and at the bottom of the pyramid the people have none. Or at least this is how it seems to those disenfranchised people who haven't been offered equitable opportunity. Understanding that you don't have power or opportunity has a huge detrimental effect on your mindset.

But what would happen if we inverted this model and put the people at the top of the pyramid, at the top of the power structure? What would happen if we structured our society in this way? How does inverting the power structure change the mindset? By placing people at the top, you acknowledge they are the most important. You empower them, allowing their needs to come first. All sorts of things would be opened up.

If we start with the people and place citizens at the top of our priorities by empowering them to participate, the mindset can adapt and shift from being pessimistic, fixed, and divided to becoming united. Empowerment will mean that people not only have a voice but have a voice that is heard and acted upon. People will feel the future is in their hands; it's theirs for the taking.

Corporations in Africa, in the middle layer, while showing promise, often fall short in terms of realizing their full potential. Many businesses operate with a short-term focus, driven by immediate profits rather than sustainable growth. By aligning corporate goals with the will of the people, businesses can deliver sustainable development and prosperity. I want to see corporations adopting the united mindset; doing so will enable them to operate to achieve more socially aware growth and prosperity. They can both learn from and support the people of Africa in this way. If more Africans have greater wealth, corporations benefit exponentially.

Political leaders in Africa can sometimes exhibit a mindset that hampers progress—a divided and at times colonial mindset. While it is my intention to support leaders, I have to call out the clear injustices I see. Corruption, lack of vision, and a tendency to prioritize personal gain over public good are significant issues in many African countries due to problems with many African leaders. However, a bigger issue than being in power for the wrong reasons is the inability to negotiate from a position of strength when it comes to funding their country's development: the divided mindset.

By putting people's views, voices, and needs first, and by being led by the will of the people, corporations and leaders operate on the mandate handed to them by the people. Being at the bottom of the power structure pyramid, they need to craft their leadership style accordingly. There is a symbiotic model in which the people empower the politicians and the politicians empower the people. In this way, the African mindset becomes united. It is not a negative for politicians to be at the bottom of the pyramid; instead, they are able to better understand and serve their citizens. It's win-win.

To bring about meaningful change, there must be an overhaul in the way political leadership operates. All leaders need to adopt a mindset of social contract, service, integrity, and strength, and all should develop a long-term vision while empowering the next generation of leaders. Even if this pyramid structure is purely theoretical, by putting the people first, by empowering their citizens, the mindset shifts at every level to become united.

Chapter 3

LEADERSHIP

When talking of leadership in Africa, my vision is that people should, in the future, only think of strong, visionary, empowering leaders and never think of the ugly impact of corruption. The good news is there is hope one day this could be the case. There are, of course, countries that have already been shaped by visionaries, their impact firmly felt by their neighbors, the wider continent, and indeed the whole world.

LEARNING FROM STRONG LEADERS

Countries like Rwanda, under President Paul Kagame, have demonstrated the impact of visionary and disciplined leadership. Kagame's focus on economic development, technology, and anti-corruption measures has led to significant progress.

For those who may be unfamiliar with him, Kagame played a crucial role in ending the Rwandan genocide in 1994. Under his leadership, Rwanda has undergone a somewhat unrecognizable transformation that is an enormous feat of achievement, changing from a nation devastated by ethnic conflict to one known for peace and stability. How did he achieve this? His policies focused on reconciliation and unity.

Kagame spearheaded economic reforms that led to impressive economic growth. Rwanda has consistently achieved high GDP growth rates, and the country has become an attractive destination for foreign investment. Kagame's administration has been noted for its strong stance against corruption. Rwanda has implemented stringent anti-corruption measures and now has a relatively low level of corruption compared to other countries in the region. With a corruption index score of 53 (in 2023),[5] the country sits above the two thirds of countries that score under 50/100, indicating serious corruption problems and putting it on par with Grenada, Georgia, and Cyprus. This has improved the business climate and increased public trust in government institutions.

Rwanda's health care system has improved, boosting life expectancy, and the education sector has also seen substantial progress, with higher student numbers and improved literacy levels. Kagame's government has been a global leader in promoting gender equality. Rwanda is the first country in the world with a female majority in parliament: With 61.3 percent in the Chamber of Deputies and 37.4 percent in the Senate it has the highest proportion of women in power worldwide.[6]

Technological innovation is a key driver of development. The establishment of innovation hubs and tech-friendly policies have encouraged entrepreneurship and digital transformation. The country has implemented policies that protect natural resources, promote sustainable agriculture, and increase forestation.

I wanted to experience Rwanda myself and was fortunate enough to be invited to the Global AI Summit on Africa, which was organized by the World Economic Forum. As participant and as a leader in business and technology, my discussions with leaders and entrepreneurs from both Africa and other continents were rich and insightful. What amazed me the most was the fact that I didn't see a single paper or plastic anywhere on the ground during my trip from the airport to the hotel and throughout my one-week visit to Kigali, capital of Rwanda. It was encouraging and inspiring to see a country make that transition successfully; it solidified my vision for Africa—impossible is nothing.

Ghana, too, is still benefitting from the strong leadership of Kwame Nkrumah in the 60s and 70s; indeed, his achievements were transformative for Ghana and Africa as a whole. He successfully mobilized mass support through his charismatic leadership, which eventually led to Ghana becoming the first African

[5] https://www.transparency.org/en/cpi/2023/index/rwa

[6] https://www.parliament.gov.rw/women-representation

country to gain independence on March 6, 1957. This inspired other African nations to pursue their own independence. Dr. Nkrumah was a staunch advocate of and worked tirelessly to promote African unity. His leadership focused on economic self-sufficiency and industrialization, with policies aimed to reduce dependence on foreign aid and promote internal development. Investing heavily in education, the University of Ghana was established to develop a skilled workforce.

Dr. Nkrumah promoted gender equality, improved health care, and expanded social services, aiming to elevate the living standards of all Ghanaians. Overall, though, it was his charisma that inspired both his compatriots and other African leaders; he became a symbol of African liberation.

However, Nkrumah's success made him a threat to Western interests, and sadly his downfall was orchestrated through external interference. As his bold vision for African self-sufficiency and unity aimed to reduce reliance on Western powers and nationalize key industries, he was seen as a direct challenge to Western economic and political dominance.

His close ties with socialist countries and his push for an independent, industrialized Africa made him a target of Cold War geopolitics. In 1966, while he was on a diplomatic trip to China and North Vietnam, a coup backed by Western intelligence agencies, particularly the CIA, overthrew his government. Declassified documents later revealed that the West saw his policies as a threat to their control over Africa's resources and influence.

For me, this raises a crucial question: Does the West deliberately keep ineffective African leaders in power? Many post-independence African leaders who conformed to Western economic interests remained in office for decades, while those who pushed for self-reliance and unity, like Nkrumah, were swiftly removed.

Another exceptional leader was Nelson Mandela. His achievements are, of course, globally celebrated and recognized. His leadership and vision played a crucial role in ending apartheid and establishing a multiracial democracy in South Africa. Mandela's path to success was long and hard, and for decades people may have reasonably given up hope. Mandela joined the

African National Congress (ANC) in 1943 and helped form the ANC Youth League, advocating nonviolent resistance against apartheid. Later, in response to increasing government repression, he advocated sabotage as a means to achieve change. He was arrested and sentenced to life imprisonment in 1964 for his anti-apartheid activities.

During his twenty-seven years in prison, he became a symbol of resistance and galvanized international support. Upon his release in 1990, Mandela led negotiations with the government to dismantle apartheid, facilitating the country's first multiracial elections in 1994 when he was elected as South Africa's first Black president. As president, he prioritized national reconciliation, promoting peace and unity among South Africa's diverse populations. He addressed past human rights abuses and fostered healing. Mr. Mandela continued to advocate for peace, human rights, and social justice and founded the Nelson Mandela Foundation to promote his vision and legacy globally.

Mandela's leadership was marked by his ability to inspire and unite people across racial and political divides. His commitment to forgiveness, reconciliation, and inclusivity set a powerful example for leaders worldwide. Mandela's resilience, moral integrity, and unwavering dedication to justice and equality solidified his status as one of the most revered leaders of the twentieth century. His legacy continues to influence and inspire those working for social justice and human rights around the world.

Mandela's leadership style and character are often cited as central to his success and influence as a great leader. Mandela had a clear vision for a free and democratic South Africa; his commitment to this vision was unwavering, and he was able to articulate it, even during twenty-seven years in jail, in a way that inspired millions of people to support and work toward it. He was widely respected for his integrity, honesty, and commitment to justice, which earned him the trust and admiration of people both within South Africa and globally. One of Mandela's most remarkable traits was his ability to forgive those who had wronged him and his people.

Mandela was a strategic thinker who was able to understand and navigate the complexities of the political landscape. He was resilient, with an ability to endure hardship without losing hope.

Despite his significant achievements, Mandela remained humble, approachable, and empathetic. He was well liked and respected around the world, and his legacy is enduring.

THE QUALITIES OF LEADERSHIP

Not all these leaders have the same leadership style. No one taught them to be great leaders; they didn't learn to be great leaders at university or study for an MBA. Instead, these men had something far more powerful and effective: They were driven by conviction and vision. Leadership was their life's work, not than a job. It was their calling.

I've worked in leadership roles myself, and I believe strong and effective leadership to be both something you can be born with and something you can learn. Some people, like Nkrumah, are natural leaders; others learn how to be great leaders. Some people have some natural talent and develop it further. And there are plenty of people who are never going to be good leaders, or leaders at all, and that's okay. Leadership is, by its very nature, not for everyone.

Leadership necessitates certain qualities. For sure, it takes a special kind of personality and the ability to win people over to your way of thinking. It requires persuasiveness, vision, courage, empathy, rigor, and tenacity. And it requires a certain amount of ego, but just the right amount to want to put yourself in the place to create great change for other people and not so much that you operate out of self-interest.

The appeal of leading a team, company, or country, however, appeals to many, so it attracts a fair few who shouldn't take up these appealing leadership roles: the power-mad people whose egos are too big, the people who see leadership as a fast track to financial wealth, and the people who don't understand that to lead you have to bring people with you and work for the people, not the other way around.

I see leaders from all walks of life leading all sorts of things, from African countries to government departments, to global businesses, to teams, to my kids' kindergarten. In each situation they need different domain expertise, but if they are to be successful leaders, they all also need the same leadership skills. And if they want to be great leaders, they need these skills in abundance.

GREAT LEADERS ARE RARE

Finding great leaders is hard, whatever the context. A key problem with leadership, as I've experienced it throughout my life, is that of entitlement. I discussed entitlement as a positive earlier, when discussing how I wanted all Africans to feel entitled to opportunity. Here, entitlement means something very different. "Entitlement to lead" is a huge problem—in politics, in business, in education, and elsewhere. Often, people feel they are entitled to become leaders through experience; they feel that they should be promoted to leadership positions simply due to their tenure in a role, company, or organization. The length of service someone has in a certain area or how much of a subject matter expert they are really bares very little relevance to how well they lead. Yet in many settings people are promoted to leadership roles for this simple unrelated fact.

And that's because, as we absolutely must acknowledge, leadership comes with perks. Often it comes with a better salary than a non-leadership, managerial, or other type of role. In many professional settings, there is a lack of a suitable structure that allows highly skilled and highly experienced people to rise through the ranks without asking them to also become leaders and then expecting them to know how to lead people into the unknown. There's simply nowhere for people to go and no way to reward them aside from appointing them as leaders, often without any leadership training whatsoever.

If we could give good people great perks, then I would hope fewer of them would feel the need to take up leadership roles in order to get appropriately compensated. We need to develop a better understanding of leadership and all it entails and ensure we attract the best and the brightest but also encourage others without those skills to work in other roles.

Entitlement to leadership can also come in the form of nepotism, either directly as people hire friends and family or by creating new leaders in the same mold as the old ones. This occurs in the absence of a fair and transparent meritocratic system. For example, by expecting that middle-aged men with university degrees who've had a career in politics are the best leaders, we will get more middle-aged men with university degrees and careers in politics leading our countries. Plenty of this cohort may be excellent leaders, but other people might be excellent leaders too. By removing all the forms of entitlement in leadership, we make sure we attract the right leaders with the right skills, or basis for nurturing their leadership skills, and, importantly, the right motivation.

There have been good and bad leaders throughout history, in all contexts; indeed, there have been good and bad leaders in modern African history. To move forward though, we need less of the old type of leadership typified by entitlement and greed. We need fewer, indeed no more, corrupt leaders at any level in African politics. I call a fresh breed of African leader "new," although in reality there have been some of these new, true leaders all along. But we need to distinguish between leaders who serve themselves and who serve us at every level. To help Africa unite and become more self-sufficient, a new kind of leadership must be characterized by several key attributes.

WE NEED LEADERS WHO CAN END CORRUPTION

To tackle corruption we need courage, humility, and passion. Then more courage, fearlessness, bravery, and strength. First, though, our leaders must be in the leadership game for the right reasons. Politicians and church leaders alike should be well rewarded, but not at the expense of their people. Transparency and accountability are crucial to combating corruption and building trust among citizens. Leaders must commit to ethical governance practices and ensure that resources are used effectively and equitably.

It is simply not acceptable to me that so many do without because so few divert funds to their own coffers. While we need to "tackle" corruption, we must tackle it with the expectation, no, with the certainty, of ending it. For the new breed of leaders across the political structure, at all levels, there can be simply no possibility of ever operating outside of the law and standards of decency. Especially in our banking systems, there are measures that can be adopted for those with the will.

WE NEED LEADERS WHO WILL HONOR THEIR SOCIAL CONTRACT

Leaders must keep their social contract with their people. This means fulfilling any and all promises they make during elections and ensuring governmental actions align with the expectations and needs of the people. When promises are kept, trust is built, and citizens are more likely to support their leaders, creating a stable and supportive environment. Failure to honor the social contract leads to disillusionment, unrest, and a breakdown in the relationship between the government and its citizens.

WE NEED LEADERS WITH A CLEAR VISION

Leaders must have a clear, long-term vision for the continent's development that transcends their own national geography or borders and transcends their own short-term political gains. We need people who are prepared to think further and bigger than themselves. We also need leaders to operate with the best intentions for the future, regardless of their term in office. Leaders must be able to articulate their vision and take people on their long-term journey.

WE NEED INCLUSIVE LEADERS

True leadership is no leadership at all if you plan on leaving any people behind, especially if you plan on leaving them behind due to a certain characteristic. Leaders should prioritize inclusive policies that consider the needs of all demographic groups to support unity and growth.

WE NEED COLLABORATIVE AND PAN-AFRICAN LEADERS

A united Africa requires leaders who can work collaboratively across borders, so we need leaders who can promote regional dialogue, cooperation, and integration. This involves making tough decisions, being experts in diplomacy, articulating a vision, and leading other leaders to unite on the global stage. This takes a special kind of leader, one who can see further than the issues solely facing their country, one who knows that strength is in unity.

WE NEED INNOVATIVE LEADERS

New African leaders must be forward looking and willing to take many leaps of faith. They will need to support the development of education, health care, and infrastructure and to diversify the African economy. They will need to innovate to boost self-sufficiency. They will need to surround themselves with knowledgeable experts and invest in propelling Africa forward.

WE NEED EMPOWERING LEADERS

The people need to nurture and harness their power in a skilled workforce by contributing to the good of their communities and responding to the rally cry of unification. While the mindset of the African people is indeed changing organically, from the bottom up, the best leaders will be those who understand they need to truly empower the people if Africa is to prosper.

Empowering the whole of society, including the all-important youth and marginalized communities, is vital for effective development. New African leaders should focus on creating opportunities for thorough employment and political participation for all. The people need to be empowered and mobilized.

WE NEED YOUNG LEADERS

We need young leaders who are aware of the challenges facing our continent and able to champion solutions. Youth bring fresh perspectives, energy, and a willingness to challenge the status quo; these are all qualities that are essential for driving Africa forward. We need young leaders to bring change, to do things differently. By empowering young leaders, we can bridge the gap between the old and new, ensuring that the future is shaped by those who will inherit it. Young leaders are not just the leaders of tomorrow; they are the leaders of today, and their involvement is crucial for building a more transparent, equitable, and prosperous Africa.

Chapter 4

LET'S COLLABORATE!

There are many people who see themselves as part of Africa's solution, key players in Africa's future. And they are indeed key players. Most of these people are politicians, civil servants, leaders—those who already have at least a small amount of power, many who already have a lot. There are, however, many more people who will be crucial to Africa's development who are not current politicians, civil servants, leaders, elite businesspeople, church leaders, and so on—people without power today. I believe we need to involve a wider cross section of people if we are to unite Africa, if Africa is to develop untethered. Why? Because the political class do things in the style of the political class: They use politics, not strategy; they are clouded by ideology, by the past, by keeping to some degree the status quo that afforded them their power.

Through this book I am hoping to define and then achieve something new. I propose to approach the problems of Africa from a strategic perspective and hope to offer solutions that can drive meaningful change without political bias or personal ego. In the corporate world, we have learned the value of empowering teams, nurturing talent, and fostering an environment where collaboration and participation are encouraged. Leadership with a small "l"—leadership that is driven not by ego but by empowerment and collective goal setting—is the cornerstone of modern, innovative, and successful organizations. I believe that these principles are not only applicable but essential for the transformation of Africa.

There are many synergies between business solutions and solutions for Africa. Just as companies diversify their product lines to mitigate risks, Africa's nations can diversify their economies to reduce dependency on a single sector. Just as corporations need robust logistics and supply chains, we can build on business best practices to develop strategies to improve transportation networks, energy supply, and digital connectivity across the continent. Just as companies invest in their employees through training and development programs to enhance productivity and innovation, Africa should adopt a similar approach. Just as collaboration between the public and private sectors can lead to innovative solutions and shared resources in a corporate setting, public–private partnerships should be developed to support growth in Africa.

My aim is not to dictate political agendas but to support Africa's political leaders with strategic insights and practical solutions. By working alongside policymakers, I'd like to offer strategies that are grounded in insight, best practices, and proven methodologies. I see my role as a catalyst for change, providing strategy to benefit the entire continent.

Collaboration is at the heart of my strategic vision for Africa. By bringing together government officials, business leaders, and community stakeholders, we can create a unified approach to development. This collaborative model ensures that all voices are heard and that solutions are tailored to the unique needs and aspirations of each African nation.

Throughout this book, I outline a series of necessary pivots that are actionable and impactful. Each pivot will be designed to address critical areas. Through these pivots, I aim to create a sustainable and prosperous future for Africa, where every citizen can thrive.

First, I will outline a vision for a United Countries of Africa, with a single currency, single passport, and open borders. Next, I look at integration of defense, education, health care and communication. I argue that by approaching these areas continentally we will be better able to support our thriving population and economies. I turn to self-sufficiency and trade and look at how Africa can learn from the likes of the UAE and China.

All of this though is through a collaborative lens and with a focus on all Africans, starting with African youth, as opposed to starting from the top with political elites. I draw a lot from my corporate, strategic experience and firmly believe that anything can be achieved with the right mindset. I have already discussed the African mindset and what needs to change. Once we harness the energy of Africa's youth and achieve a shift toward a united mindset, any of these pivots, any of these ideas, however large and complex, can happen if we have the will, if we collaborate.

SECTION 2

WHERE IS AFRICA'S SCHENGEN?

Chapter 5

WHAT IF AFRICA WERE THE "UNITED COUNTRIES OF AFRICA"?

Now I'd like to delve into perhaps the most audacious question one could ask about Africa. Imagine, for a moment, Africa unified as a single nation. What would Africa look like if it were a single, united country?

Why is this so audacious? Why is it ambitious and even risky to propose such an idea? It's audacious because it challenges the deeply entrenched political, social, and economic structures that have defined the continent for centuries. It also requires a radical transformation and unprecedented levels of cooperation and compromise among Africa's fifty-four nations. It is ambitious because it aims to unify a continent that has been fragmented by colonial borders, ethnic conflicts, divergent political systems, and, of course, corruption. Proposing a united Africa is not to be taken lightly. I am fully aware of what it would require: wholesale change in approach to leadership and government and, importantly, a drastic shift in mindset.

African leaders would need to relinquish a degree of, but of course not all, sovereignty to a single centralized government. And while I do not propose *all* government be centralized, the political establishment may currently be reluctant to cede *any* control over their national affairs. Economic disparity among African countries poses a significant obstacle; wealthier nations may be hesitant to share resources. Culture, language, security concerns, and the huge economic disparity among some African nations further complicate this vision.

Despite these challenges, though, the vision of a United Countries of Africa (UCoA) is appealing because it offers such transformative potential. In my mind, it promises to elevate Africa's global standing, making it a powerful player on the world stage; Africa would experience less poverty and disease and greater economic growth, stability, development, and prosperity.

Proposing a United Countries of Africa is audacious and ambitious because it challenges the status quo and envisions a radically different future. It's also audacious for me to suggest it because it's not a new idea. I am not pretending it's new. Others have suggested it, evangelized it, and tried it but not fully succeeded at bringing it about. I am proposing a United Countries of Africa because I genuinely believe it is the right approach for the continent; I believe it has Africa's best interests at heart, and I believe it can be achieved.

A BRIEF HISTORY OF A UNITED AFRICA

The "What if Africa were one nation?" question often gets sidelined because its vision seems overwhelmingly ambitious, and the implications are extraordinarily complex. However, this shouldn't deter us from seriously contemplating the immense power and potential Africa could harness if it were united. Too often, we shy away from pondering the extraordinary impact such unity could bring, dismissing it as a mere dream. But what if we dared to dream a little longer and think a little deeper about this outlandish idea?

The concept of a united Africa has been a recurring theme, at least throughout recent history, championed by visionaries who saw the immense potential of a continent unified both politically and economically. One of the earliest and most passionate advocates was Dr. Kwame Nkrumah, Ghana's first president. In the late 1950s and early 1960s, Nkrumah's vision for Pan-Africanism was not just about independence from colonial rule; it was about creating a robust, self-sufficient Africa. His rallying cry, "Africa must unite," resonated deeply with those who dreamed of a continent with a continental government, a common defense system, and a unified economic strategy. When visiting Ghana, I remember feeling the palpable legacy of Nkrumah's aspirations in the air. There was a sense of pride and potential that was almost tangible.

Julius Nyerere, the first president of Tanzania, was another proponent of the united Africa vision. Like Nkrumah, he believed that unity was the key to political stability and economic development. Nyerere's advocacy for a Pan-African federation and his support for regional integration efforts were driven by a genuine belief in the power of collective strength. Nyerere's ideas still influence discussions about regional cooperation and unity.

The formation of the Organization of African Unity (OAU) in 1963 was a big milestone in this journey. The OAU aimed to promote unity and solidarity among African states, coordinate cooperation, and defend sovereignty. However, it stopped short of creating a single political entity. I've often wondered how different the continent might look today if the OAU had been able to push further toward true political union.

Despite the enthusiasm and efforts of these leaders, the dream of a fully united Africa has remained elusive. The African Union, which replaced the OAU in 2002, continues to strive for greater integration and cooperation. The AU has made strides in promoting peace, security, and economic cooperation, but achieving the level of unity envisioned by Nkrumah and Nyerere remains a complex and gradual process.

I remain hopeful, however, that with persistent effort and visionary leadership the dream of a united Africa could become a reality. I believe a united Africa is the best way forward for the continent and that, given enough focus, there is a chance it could happen.

If African leaders, businesses, and people all believe it's too much of a pipe dream, then indeed it'll never happen. If, on the other hand, we can foster a change mindset, then anything is possible.

WHY AFRICA IS NOT UNITED TODAY

Of course, Africa is a diverse continent with diverse countries, economies, political systems, religions, languages, cultures, and people. This makes it rich, but also complex. Putting a desire for local sovereignty aside, it is economic disparity that makes a united Africa particularly difficult. The varying levels of development, resources, and economic policies make it challenging to create a unified system that benefits all member states equally. I've sat in meetings when these disparities were starkly evident, and the task of finding a middle ground seemed herculean.

Ongoing conflicts and political instability in various parts of Africa have also hampered efforts to achieve unity. Conflicts create an environment where unity seems like a distant dream. The reluctance of many African leaders to cede national sovereignty to a continental government is another significant barrier. I've had conversations with officials who are fiercely protective of their national autonomy, viewing it as essential to their country's identity and control over resources. Yet I believe there is a glimmer of hope as many I speak to wholeheartedly understand the benefits of unification, despite their desire to protect their nation's sovereignty.

External powers have historically influenced African politics and economics, often discouraging unity to maintain their interests in the continent. This external interference is something I've also witnessed in various forms, from subtle diplomatic pressures to more overt economic manipulations. That's why it is even more imperative that Africa unite to take its place on the world stage and come together as bigger than the already sizeable sum of its parts.

MY VISION FOR A UNITED COUNTRIES OF AFRICA

Imagine a continent where fifty-four diverse nations come together united in purpose and vision. What if Africa became a single entity, with one diplomatic voice on the world stage? What if the United Countries of Africa had open borders, a unified government, a single currency, and one passport for all its citizens?

I would go so far as to propose that this is the only way forward for Africa in order to properly protect itself, take its place on the world stage, provide for its people, and harness and realize its true potential. Africa must have a central government (albeit supported by local country-specific governments), open borders, the free movement of people between countries, free trade between African nations, a single currency, a single communications system and country code, and a single passport available to all its citizens.

IMAGINE THE UNITED COUNTRIES OF AFRICA IN 2050

Imagine with me, for a moment, what life would be like. By 2050, I imagine waking up in a hotel in Cairo, Egypt, and starting my day with a quick glance at the international news, which highlights the UCoA's collaboration with global superpowers.

I am heading home to a crucial conference in Accra focused on defense technology, a sector where I am meeting with business leaders and investors. With the UCoA's seamless travel system and single passport policy, moving between countries is effortless. I book my flight with ease knowing that my digital passport will streamline the entire process. Our single crypto-based currency eliminates any concerns about currency exchange, making travel even simpler.

Arriving at Cairo International Airport, the efficiency is impressive. Biometric scans replace traditional checks, and I am through to my gate in no time. Boarding the plane, I reflect on how far we have come from the days of complicated visa applications and long airport lines. The flight to Accra is smooth, and I spend the time reading about the latest innovations in our unified defense system, which integrates cutting-edge technology from across the continent.

Touching down in Accra, I am welcomed by colleagues from various UCoA member states. Our conference is set to take place in one of Accra's modern convention centers, a well-known symbol of the city's rapid development and the continent's progress. Discussions center around leveraging our collective defense capabilities to enhance security and stability across Africa. The unified defense system has not only improved our ability to protect our borders but has also fostered a sense of shared responsibility and collaboration among African nations. The conference celebrates the fact there is very little conflict in Africa in 2050, compared to twenty-five years before.

Accra itself is vibrant and bustling, a testament to the economic growth spurred by the UCoA's policies. Businesses thrive under the stability provided by a single currency and simpler, trade-friendly regulations.

In the evening, I attend a virtual meeting with representatives from the European Union and the United States. The UCoA's strong, unified voice in these discussions is evident. Our collective stance has given us significant leverage in international negotiations, ensuring that Africa's interests are represented and respected.

The meeting includes discussions on joint initiatives to combat cyberthreats and enhance global security. The UCoA's advanced defense technology is now being integrated with allies' systems to create a more secure global network. This partnership underscores the importance of Africa on the world stage and our ability to contribute significantly to global security. The UCoA has facilitated not only economic growth but also a sense of unity and shared purpose among Africans, especially Africa's youth, who have enjoyed exponentially better educational opportunities in the last twenty-five years.

THE BENEFITS OF A UNITED AFRICA

Before we address how to achieve some of these highly ambitious components of a united Africa, I want to dwell on the benefits – see table 1.

Table 1. Components of a United Africa

Government	Imagine a unified Africa governed by a central government that respects and supports the unique needs of individual countries. This could unlock the unprecedented potential of a prosperous continent. A central government would streamline decision-making processes and eliminate the bureaucratic delays and inconsistencies that often arise from having multiple, independent governments. Efficiencies from centralization are clear to all, and all African citizens enjoy more streamlined government.
Economics	A unified economic policy could harmonize trade regulations, tariffs, and taxation, creating a seamless market for goods and services. This would attract foreign investment and stimulate intra-African trade, boosting economic growth and creating jobs.
Single Voice	Africa could leverage its collective bargaining power on the global stage, securing better trade deals and fostering stronger economic partnerships with other regions.
Infrastructure	A central government could coordinate large-scale infrastructure projects that span multiple countries, ensuring resources are allocated efficiently and projects are completed on time and to budget. Projects such as trans-African railways, highways, and energy grids would become more feasible, connecting remote areas and boosting the continental economy.
Education	A unified approach to education would be transformative and would be more feasible under a centralized government. A central government could ensure that all Africans have access to quality education and could develop the skills Africa needs to thrive.
Health	A central government could oversee Africa-wide health care, reducing disparities between countries and regions, promoting health equality, and preventing disease. A central government would be better able to respond to health crises such as pandemics, not only saving but also enriching lives.

Continued

Table 1. Continued

Environment	A central government could address environmental issues, such as deforestation, water management, and conservation, to protect Africa's rich biodiversity for future generations.
Defense	Security and defense would be significantly enhanced under a central government, creating a safer future for all. Political stability would be a critical advantage. A central government could mediate conflicts and foster cooperation, reducing the risk of conflict and unrest.
Cybersecurity	Centralized cybersecurity capability would be a key benefit. The threat of cyberattacks looms large, with the potential to disrupt economies, compromise personal data, and threaten national security. A centralized cybersecurity framework would allow African nations to pool resources, share intelligence, and develop robust defense mechanisms against cyberthreats. A collective approach would enhance the security of digital infrastructures, protect sensitive information, and ensure the continuity of essential services.
Communications	Shared government communications would streamline governance and improve the efficiency of public services. With a unified platform, governments across Africa could coordinate more effectively, implement policies uniformly, and respond more effectively to crises. This not only enhances the delivery of public services but also fosters greater transparency and accountability.
Country Code	Just as the US has +1, I would welcome a single code for Africa. This would be more than just a convenience; it would symbolize a collective identity and a commitment to shared technological progress.
Currency	A single currency would enable better trade and economic stability, boost tourism, and, more importantly, accelerate meeting the never-ending and unfair obligations of the IMF.

LOCAL GOVERNMENT

While a central government would oversee broad policies and initiatives, it would still support country-specific local governments. This would ensure the unique needs and preferences of individual countries are respected and addressed. Local governments would handle day-to-day governance, maintaining a sense of autonomy and local cultural identity within the broader framework of a unified Africa.

GREATER GOOD

I believe all Africans would be better off in a united Africa. Yet bringing such a structure about, against the backdrop of diverse economic climates across Africa, will be hard. To achieve this vision, we need a new breed of leadership, a new breed of leaders who can put aside personal gain and tribal issues for the overwhelmingly greater good. I will discuss leadership later in this book; of course, leadership is indeed key to any transformation. While most people accept this vision is good for everyone, it will take a special kind of leader to bring it about. Africa prospers together.

A UNITED AFRICA IS NOT IN EVERYONE'S INTEREST

Unity would be good for Africa, but is it good for everyone? Is it good for other countries? You might imagine that when everyone prospers, everyone indeed prospers. And you might also imagine everyone in every nation would naturally support Africa's development, that they would naturally cheerlead Africa's growth, stability, and prosperity. Sadly, however, there are reasons other countries not only benefit from Africa sticking with the status quo but actually benefit from Africa being divided. I find this tragic, but it's vital to understand when exploring why Africa doesn't have more support and encouragement to unite.

China, the United States, some European nations, and others have significant economic interests in Africa. Such countries benefit from dealing with individual countries that lack the bargaining power of a united continent. Dealing individually on a nation-by-nation basis allows them to secure better terms for access to natural resources, trade agreements, and investment opportunities. Whereas a united Africa could negotiate as a global power, individual countries, even the larger ones, simply aren't going to have enough bargaining power. A divided Africa therefore makes it easier for some countries to gain access to resources like oil, gas, minerals, and agricultural products at the lowest price possible. On one end of the scale, this is simply driving a hard bargain, but at the other end of the scale, this could be exploitation.

Some countries, including the United States and some European countries, also maintain strategic military influence in Africa and some maintain military bases. A fragmented Africa allows these countries to establish and maintain military presences in key regions, where they can conduct counterterrorism operations and safeguard maritime routes. A united Africa, on the other hand, while not necessarily evicting such a presence, might negotiate better terms. It would certainly act differently in unison.

Many countries also cultivate political alliances with individual African nations to gain support in international organizations like the United Nations. Traditionally, this may have been limited to Western powers, but it now also includes Russia and China. By offering development aid, military assistance, or diplomatic support, they can secure votes and influence on global issues. A united Africa with a single diplomatic voice would be much harder to sway and could present a more formidable bloc in international diplomacy.

Countries like Russia benefit further from a divided Africa by extending their influence through military cooperation, arms sales, and political alliances. Russia has been able to gain strategic footholds in regions where Western influence is waning. A fragmented Africa allows countries like Russia to compete more effectively against its rivals, using African nations as pawns in broader geopolitical struggles.

Plenty of countries and international organizations provide humanitarian and development aid to African nations. While aid is often well-intentioned, it can also be a tool for maintaining influence. A united Africa might seek more equitable terms or collective negotiations that could reduce the leverage of donor countries.

And finally is trade and investment: Countries like China have invested heavily in African infrastructure and development projects. By dealing with individual nations, China has negotiated terms that often include resource-for-infrastructure deals, which might be less favorable in a united Africa with a stronger collective power base. Similarly, European countries benefit from preferential trade agreements with individual African nations that might be renegotiated by a unified Africa. There are many reasons that other nations would be fearful of Africa uniting. The biggest reason is, of course, economics: Things would simply start to cost them more.

So, do other nations seek to keep Africa divided? Well, I think it's more subtle than that. While nations that trade with and invest in Africa contribute to its development, there are also mechanics for the same nations to hold Africa back. As I discuss later in this book, the IMF is instrumental in determining the wealth of African nations and African people. Many of the nations who'd lose the most from Africa uniting are those with the most influence on the IMF. They're the ones contributing to setting the policies that keep Africa operating in a certain way. And while African nations are struggling to repay IMF debt, they're not focused on the best strategies for development. They're not focused on creating a united Africa that has more sway on the global stage.

Chapter 6

WHAT IF AFRICA HAD OPEN BORDERS AND A SINGLE PASSPORT?

If Africa were the United Countries of Africa, it would of course need open borders and a single passport. But these interconnected ideas wouldn't just encourage more Africans to travel; they could also solve employment and skills issues by making African skills and labor more accessible across the continent.

A single passport, perhaps called the UCoA Pass, would foster a sense of unity and unlock immense economic and social benefits. It would allow all Africans to move between countries with ease, requiring and facilitating open borders. Imagine an Africa where borders are merely lines on a map that respect cultural sovereignty rather than barriers to opportunity. In such an Africa, individuals could move freely, living and working in any country, and be on the path to prosperity and unity.

One of the most profound benefits of open borders would be the seamless movement of people across the continent. Lengthy, bureaucratic visa applications and border restrictions would be a thing of the past. Africans could travel freely, seizing new opportunities for work, education, and leisure. This freedom of movement would enable individuals to pursue jobs that match their skills, regardless of location, leading to a more efficient and dynamic labor market. The ability to relocate easily would also help alleviate unemployment and underemployment, as people could move to areas with greater demand for their expertise.

Open borders would significantly enhance trade and commerce. Without stringent border controls and tariffs, businesses could operate more smoothly, cutting down on costs and delays. The ease of moving goods and services across borders would make African businesses more competitive globally, as businesses could expand their operations with ease. Entrepreneurs would be able to tap into new markets, form partnerships, and establish operations in different countries without bureaucratic hurdles. This openness would encourage investment and stimulate innovation. The reduction in trade barriers would lower costs, making African products more competitive on the global stage.

Increased mobility could lead to the development of regional hubs of excellence, with cities specializing in different industries and becoming centers of innovation. Imagine Lagos as a technology hub, Nairobi as a center for education and research, Johannesburg as a financial powerhouse, and Accra as a manufacturing mecca.

Education would be transformed. Students could attend universities in different African countries without worrying about visa restrictions or residency requirements. Access to diverse education would enrich learning and better prepare students for the demands of the globalized world. The exchange of knowledge and ideas among students from various backgrounds would foster a generation of leaders who are not only skilled but also culturally and globally aware.

Access to health care would improve dramatically with a single African passport and open borders. People in regions with limited facilities could travel to neighboring countries with better health care systems. This mobility could save lives and ensure that more Africans receive the medical attention they need. In emergencies, the ability to cross borders without restrictions could make all the difference.

Tourism would flourish as Africans explore their continent without the need for visa applications. A boost in domestic tourism would create jobs and support local economies.

Instead of a loss of sovereignty, a single African passport would symbolize a commitment to unity and cooperation, underpinning the open border policy. It would necessitate and enable greater collaboration on security and immigration policies and encourage intelligence sharing to combat terrorism and crime.

A united approach would create a more peaceful continent. The single passport would be a tangible representation of Pan-African identity, fostering pride and solidarity among citizens. It would promote inclusivity and mutual respect as people from different backgrounds and regions interact more freely and frequently. An African passport wouldn't just be a travel document but a powerful tool for economic, social, and political transformation, focused on driving growth and prosperity for all.

Chapter 7

WHAT IF AFRICA HAD A SINGLE CURRENCY?

A single currency has the potential to be transformative for Africa; however, unlike the euro, which simply replaced sovereign currencies in Europe, I would propose a new African cryptocurrency because cryptocurrency offers additional benefits over fiat currency.

First, a primer on the complex state of currency in Africa. There are currently approximately forty-two different currencies in use across the fifty-four countries in Africa. The exact number is approximate and in flux for a variety of reasons. Some countries have multiple currencies; other nations share currencies with others. Other nations also count foreign currencies, including the US dollar, as accepted currencies.

The CFA Franc, for example, is a currency used in two regions of Africa, both of which are former French colonies. There are two distinct currencies known as the CFA Franc, each of which is guaranteed by the French treasury and pegged to the euro. As I write this book, the SAHEL (Mali, Burkina Faso, and Niger) has been created with its central bank and actively working on a common currency.

The West African CFA franc is used by the eight countries in the West African Economic and Monetary Union (WAEMU): Benin, Burkina Faso, Côte d'Ivoire, Guinea-Bissau, Mali, Niger, Senegal, and Togo. The Central African CFA franc is used by the six countries in the Central African Economic and Monetary

Community (CEMAC): Cameroon, the Central African Republic, Chad, the Republic of Congo, Equatorial Guinea, and Gabon.

Both the West African and Central African CFA francs are essentially separate currencies, but they are both referred to as the CFA franc and have the same value against the euro. The CFA franc was introduced during the colonial period and is still used to maintain monetary stability in the region. However, it has also been a subject of controversy and debate due to its ties to France and the limitations it places on the monetary policies of the member countries.

Already, you're understanding why currency in Africa is complex. It's not just African nations with different currencies; it's African nations and groups of African nations with currencies supported by non-African countries and linked to entirely different monetary systems. The headline is that African money is not controlled solely by Africa—far from it.

THE HISTORY OF A SINGLE AFRICAN CURRENCY

There have been several attempts to create a single African currency. The idea has been promoted by the African Union and other regional organizations for many years. The most notable effort is the African Monetary Union (AMU), which aims to establish a single currency for the entire continent by 2028, administered by the African Central Bank. This initiative is part of the broader vision outlined in the Abuja Treaty of 1991, which set the groundwork for economic integration in Africa.

The path to a single currency is to establish various regional monetary unions first, before they can then be joined in one. Africa's monetary landscape is characterized by a diverse set of currencies and regional monetary blocs. These blocs aim to facilitate economic integration, stability, and growth among member countries. Here are the five key monetary blocs already established in Africa – see table 2.

Table 2. Five Key Monetary Blocs

The West African Monetary Zone (WAMZ)	The Gambia, Ghana, Guinea, Liberia, Nigeria, and Sierra Leone.	WAMZ was established with the goal of introducing a common currency called the "Eco." The Eco aims to enhance economic integration and stability within the region. In May 2020, a significant milestone was reached when the French government and eight West African countries agreed to transition from the CFA franc to the Eco. However, by January 2021, no concrete plan had been established to bring this about. The pandemic of course impacted progress, and in 2021 the WAMZ adopted a revised plan, setting a new target to launch the Eco by 2027. However, many, including the WAMZ, feel that 2027 is unrealistic.
The West African Economic and Monetary Union (WAEMU)	Benin, Burkina Faso, Côte d'Ivoire, Guinea-Bissau, Mali, Niger, Senegal, and Togo	These countries share a common currency, the CFA franc, which is pegged to the euro and guaranteed by the French Treasury. WAEMU aims to ensure economic stability, facilitate trade, and promote economic integration among member states through a unified monetary policy and financial system.

Continued

Table 2. Continued

The Central African Economic and Monetary Community (CAEMC)	Cameroon, Central African Republic, Chad, Republic of Congo, Equatorial Guinea, and Gabon	Similar to WAEMU, CAEMC countries use the CFA franc, which is also pegged to the euro and guaranteed by the French Treasury. CAEMC's objectives include promoting economic cooperation, ensuring monetary stability, and facilitating regional trade and investment.
The Southern African Development Community (SADC)	Angola, Botswana, Comoros, Democratic Republic of Congo, Eswatini (Swaziland), Lesotho, Madagascar, Malawi, Mauritius, Mozambique, Namibia, Seychelles, South Africa, Tanzania, Zambia, and Zimbabwe	While SADC does not have a common currency, it aims to achieve economic integration through harmonized policies, free trade, and monetary cooperation. South Africa, as the region's largest economy, plays a significant role in SADC's economic activities.
The East African Community (EAC)	Burundi, Kenya, Rwanda, South Sudan, Tanzania, and Uganda	The EAC has ambitious plans to achieve deeper economic integration, including the introduction of a common currency. The bloc has made significant progress toward monetary union, including establishing a regional central bank.

These monetary blocs all aim to achieve greater economic integration, stability, and development. Each bloc faces unique challenges and opportunities, but collectively they work toward the common goal of fostering economic growth and prosperity in Africa.

There is progress, but many feel it's not enough. Leaders are increasingly calling for a single currency. In 2023 Kenya's president, William Ruto, called for a single currency: "Our people cannot trade without worrying about which currency to use. This, among other non-tariff barriers, is something we must urgently address so that our people can begin to trade together and integrate."[7]

And on the way to a single currency, many are hoping to speed up the adoption of regional monetary unions. In 2023 Ghana's vice president, Dr. Mahamudu Bawumia, urged the member states of the WAMZ to double their efforts toward meeting the macroeconomic convergence criteria for a single currency by January 2027.[8]

Of course, not all African countries are ready to join a single currency. Many, especially those in conflict, would need to make significant changes before they are able to join a new monetary union. But the carrot of unity could be offered to encourage those nations to more rapidly advance their development, peace, and stability. The prize of unity would indeed be worth working toward.

WE NEED FEWER CURRENCIES, NOT MORE

It's important to understand just how much is involved in enabling a single currency so that we can appreciate the size of the ask. Today, some African nations have more than one currency in circulation. While this may seem alien to readers in Western nations, in Africa and in developing nations it is commonplace. It usually happens in cases of economic instability, high inflation, or lack of confidence in the national currency and often leads people and businesses to use alternative currencies, especially foreign ones, for transactions.

---

[7] https://www.aa.com.tr/en/africa/kenyas-president-ruto-proposes-single-currency-for-africa/2918003

[8] https://gna.org.gh/2023/09/lets-double-our-efforts-towards-a-single-currency-by-2027-veep-to-wamz-member-states/

Zimbabwe has experienced severe hyperinflation, which led to the abandonment of the Zimbabwean dollar in 2009. Since then, multiple currencies, including the US dollar, South African rand, British pound, and the Botswana pula, have been used. In 2019, Zimbabwe reintroduced the Zimbabwean dollar, but other currencies continue to be widely used.

In Somalia, the Somali shilling is used alongside US dollars. In some areas, the Ethiopian birr and the Kenyan shilling are also used, especially in border regions. After gaining independence from Sudan in 2011, South Sudan introduced its own currency, the South Sudanese pound. However, due to ongoing conflict and economic challenges, the US dollar is also widely used.

The use of multiple currencies often reflects previous attempts to stabilize the economy, protect against inflation, and facilitate trade and investment. However, it also complicates monetary policy. A unified currency would be a stabilizing, simplifying force. And I think it should be cryptocurrency.

M-PESA: BANKING THE UNBANKED WITH MOBILE MONEY

Before I look at why cryptocurrency is beneficial to Africa, it's important to acknowledge the role of early Fintech innovation in the form of M-PESA: a mobile money transfer and micro-financing service that was originally launched in Kenya by Safaricom. Since its inception, M-PESA has expanded and is now available in seven African countries, including the Democratic Republic of Congo, Egypt, Ghana, Kenya, Lesotho, Mozambique, and Tanzania. It serves more than 51 million customers via over six hundred thousand agents. According to Vodafone, which is a part owner of Safaricom, M-PESA is used to transact over $314 billion a year.

Over 30 million Kenyans use M-PESA for daily transactions, apparently lifting 2 percent of the population out of poverty.[9]

[9] https://www.mckinsey.com/industries/financial-services/our-insights/driven-by-purpose-15-years-of-m-pesas-evolution

It's currently the most widely used services for money transfers into Africa. M-PESA users register with one of the networks of over 600,000 agents, where they can deposit and withdraw cash. Sending money is all done via the phone. Services like M-Shwari that allow users to apply for short-term micro loans are built on top of M-PESA.

Indeed, M-PESA has become a platform for numerous financial services, enhancing financial inclusion. Some of the key services built on top of M-Pesa include those listed in the following table 3.

Table 3. Key Services of M-Pesa Platform

M-Shwari	A service allowing users to save money, earn interest, and access instant micro loans
Fuliza	An overdraft facility that lets users complete transactions even without sufficient funds
KCB M-PESA	A savings accounts and instant loans service
Lipa Na M-PESA	A service that enables businesses to receive payments from customers
M-Tiba	A health wallet that allows users to save and spend funds for health care needs
M-Kopa	A pay-as-you-go solar energy solution that uses M-PESA for payments
M-Akiba	A mobile-based government bond that allows Kenyans to invest in government securities using M-PESA
Insurance	Insurance product availability, such as life, health, and crop insurance

These services have significantly expanded the reach of mobile financial services, delivering greater financial inclusion and accessibility for millions of users and thus should be seen as positive.

M-PESA VERSUS CRYPTOCURRENCY

M-PESA and its owners have not been keen to support the rise of cryptocurrency in Africa. Kipochi, a wallet and exchange that could make converting between Bitcoin and M-PESA fast, secure, and convenient, was forced to shut down after Safaricom (the company behind M-PESA) pushed their payment processor, Kopo Kopo, to cease the service.[10]

Safaricom has occasionally imposed restrictions on cryptocurrency transactions, including blocking transactions related to cryptocurrency exchanges and disallowing the use of M-PESA for buying or selling cryptocurrencies. These actions are often described as being driven by regulatory concerns, as financial authorities in various African countries have expressed apprehensions about the risks associated with cryptocurrencies. While cryptocurrencies may come with risks, I believe the benefits far outweigh the risks. Cryptocurrency is traceable; you can know about every single transaction, so citizens and businesses are protected. Plus, by the time such a scheme could be implemented, far more people across Africa would have access to the relevant technology and infrastructure required to make use of it.

M-PESA's dominance in the mobile money market in Africa, however, means it has a vested interest in maintaining its competitive edge. The rise of cryptocurrencies could pose a threat to its business model by offering alternative financial solutions to a continent just starting to benefit from a Fintech revolution.

Cryptocurrencies also pose a significant threat—not to people or business or trade, but to corruption itself. Imagine the impact of being able to track every single transaction. This would greatly reduce corrupt practices, bribes, and backhanders. It would make such activities pretty much impossible, or at the very least it would make them transparent. While a huge opportunity for African citizens, crypto certainly poses challenges for anyone who wishes corruption to remain part of doing business in Africa.

[10] https://medium.com/thedarkside/m-pesa-has-stood-in-cryptos-way-4072db0f9550

CRYPTO OUTSIDE OF GOVERNMENT CONTROL

Cryptocurrency has already been adopted by plenty of Africans, driven by a combination of economics, innovation, and opportunism.

Nigeria is one of the leading countries in Africa for cryptocurrency adoption. Despite a ban on crypto transactions within the banking sector by the Central Bank of Nigeria, Nigerians use cryptocurrencies extensively for remittances, savings, and investments. Peer-to-peer trading platforms have become particularly popular in circumventing banking restrictions.

South Africa's tech-savvy population has shown significant interest in crypto. Kenyans are using cryptocurrencies for investment and remittances and as an alternative to traditional banking services alongside M-PESA. Uganda has emerged as a hub for cryptocurrency activity in East Africa, and Zimbabweans have turned to cryptocurrencies as a hedge against hyperinflation and economic instability. Across Africa, Africans are using cryptocurrencies, whether their governments like it or not.

OFFICIAL CRYPTO IN CAR

While most governments are weary of crypto, others are more innovative. In April 2022, the Central African Republic became the second country in the world, after El Salvador, to adopt Bitcoin as legal tender. The bold move positioned the CAR at the forefront of cryptocurrency adoption in Africa. They integrated Bitcoin into the country's financial system, offering an alternative to traditional fiat currencies in a move to improve financial inclusion.

The move was driven by several factors. First, the country's financial infrastructure is underdeveloped, with a significant portion of the population lacking access to traditional banking services. By adopting Bitcoin, the CAR government hoped to provide a more accessible financial system, enabling residents to participate in the global economy through digital transactions.

CAR's economy faced challenges, including political instability and a reliance on informal sectors, so the introduction of Bitcoin was seen as a way to attract foreign investment and stimulate economic growth. Of course, the move also brought about several challenges. The CAR's internet penetration is relatively low, which could hinder widespread adoption. Additionally, there are concerns about the volatility of cryptocurrencies, which can lead to significant fluctuations in value. Critics argue that the focus on cryptocurrency might divert attention from other pressing economic and social issues.

A THIRD WAY: THE CENTRAL BANK DIGITAL CURRENCY

The lack of a robust regulatory framework for digital currencies anywhere, in Africa and globally, raises concerns about financial stability. A compromise strategy gaining popularity is the concept of the CBDC, or central bank digital currency.

A CBDC is a digital form of fiat money issued by a country's central bank. Unlike cryptocurrencies such as Bitcoin, which are decentralized and operate on blockchain technology without a central authority, a CBDC is centralized and managed by the central bank of the issuing country. While both are digital currencies, there are key differences between CBDCs and cryptocurrencies.

CBDCs are issued and controlled by a central authority, typically a nation's central bank. This means they have the backing and regulation of the government. Cryptocurrencies, on the other hand, are created and managed through decentralized networks, using blockchain technology, without central oversight. CBDCs are considered legal tender and are recognized as an official form of currency by the government.

The value of a CBDC is typically stable and pegged to the value of the national fiat currency. For example, a digital dollar would have the same value as a physical dollar, whereas cryptocurrencies can be volatile, their value fluctuating based on market demand, investor sentiment, and other global factors.

Both CBDCs and cryptocurrencies can use blockchain or other distributed ledger technologies, but CBDCs are more likely to employ private or permissioned blockchains to maintain control and oversight. Cryptocurrencies typically use public, permission-less blockchains, which allow anyone to participate and verify transactions.

CBDCs are likely to have less anonymity compared to cryptocurrencies. Central banks can track and monitor transactions made with CBDCs, which can aid in preventing illegal activities such as money laundering, fraud, and of course the diversion of public funds into private wealth.

CBDCs can complement existing fiat currency systems and can be used for everyday transactions, aiming to increase efficiency and reduce costs in the payment system. Cryptocurrencies have broader use cases, including serving as a store of value, facilitating smart contracts, and providing financial services to the unbanked, often operating outside traditional financial systems. While both CBDCs and cryptocurrencies represent digital forms of currency, their fundamental differences lie in their issuance, control, legal status, stability, technology, privacy, and intended use cases. CBDCs aim to bring the benefits of digital currency under the regulatory framework of central banks, whereas cryptocurrencies promote decentralization and operate independently of traditional financial institutions.

THE E-CEDI CBDC IN GHANA

Ghana's central bank, the Bank of Ghana, has been proactive in exploring the development of a CBDC—the e-cedi, which represents a significant step toward more integrated digital financial solutions. The central bank aimed to create a digital version of the Ghanaian cedi that would be accessible to all segments of the population, including those without traditional banking access. The goal is to provide a secure, efficient, and easily accessible means of payment that complements existing financial infrastructure.

In 2021, the Bank of Ghana partnered with the German company Giesecke+Devrient to pilot the e-cedi. The pilot phase included both offline and online capabilities, ensuring that the e-cedi could be used even in areas with limited internet connectivity; offline was important, as 47 percent of Ghanaians had no access to the internet by the start of 2022. By providing a digital currency that can be accessed via mobile phones and other digital devices, the e-cedi aimed to bring more people into the formal financial system, making it easier for them to save, invest, and conduct transactions.

Importantly, a digital currency provides a central bank with better tools to track money flows and implement policy measures more effectively. This can help in managing inflation, controlling the money supply, and ensuring economic stability.

Despite the potential benefits, the implementation of the e-cedi also faces challenges. Ensuring the security and privacy of digital transactions is paramount. Widespread adoption of the e-cedi will require substantial efforts in public education and building trust in the new digital currency.

CBDC VERSUS CRYPTO

While I am wholly supportive of moves by various African nations to implement their own CBDCs to bank the unbanked, reach remote areas, and boost prosperity and growth, I still believe that a single cryptocurrency is right for Africa. First, CBDCs are not appropriate because of the fluctuation between the various currencies of fifty-four African nations. Second, while I support countries' ability to track transactions in a bid to manage monetary policy, I am a believer in privacy and freedom, and therefore individual citizens' money should be managed away from the state. Here are my reasons for advocating a single cryptocurrency for Africa:

- A single cryptocurrency could foster economic integration across the continent. Imagine a seamless economic environment where exchange rate volatility is minimized, leading to smoother and more predictable cross-border trade.

- Cryptocurrencies typically offer lower transaction fees compared to traditional banking systems. It would make financial transactions more affordable and particularly beneficial for small- and medium-sized enterprises, supporting entrepreneurship.
- A single cryptocurrency would enhance financial inclusion by providing access to financial services for the unbanked and underbanked populations.
- Transactions recorded on a blockchain are immutable and traceable, reducing the opportunities for fraud and corruption. Increased transparency would foster a more reliable and accountable economic environment.
- People would be empowered by greater control over their financial transactions. The entrepreneurial spirit that defines Africa could further flourish with the right financial tools.
- A single cryptocurrency would streamline the process of sending and receiving money from abroad, making it faster and cheaper. Imagine families receiving money in real time, without the high costs and delays associated with traditional money transfer services.
- The adoption of a single cryptocurrency would spur tech innovation across the continent. As businesses and governments adapt to the new financial ecosystem, there would likely be an increase in the development of blockchain-based applications and services. This innovation could lead to the growth of new industries and job creation.

A single currency would change the lives of all Africans for the better.

SECTION 3

UNPRECEDENTED INTEGRATION

Chapter 8

WHAT IF AFRICA HAD A UNIFIED DEFENSE SYSTEM?

Simplistically perhaps, I would like to be able to imagine Africa is protected by a unified defense system. Such a system would protect African nations from external threats and keep regional peace. I'm sure most would agree that establishing such a system would be an important achievement that could transform the continent into a bastion of stability and cooperation.

A shared command structure in which resources, intelligence, and military capabilities are pooled together for the collective security of all member states would not only fortify the continent's defenses against external threats but unify nations, in turn protecting them from local conflict. The result would also allow Africa to negotiate with a single and powerful voice internationally.

CONFLICT TODAY

To understand why Africa doesn't have a unified defense system, and why such an idea would indeed be a big stretch, we need to understand a bit about the current state of African conflict. At the time of writing this book, there are many conflicts across Africa. The conflicts are serious, diverse, and deadly. And, sadly, while they are big news to many Africans, they often attract little attention globally.

In Ethiopia's Tigray region, conflict involving the federal government and the Tigray People's Liberation Front has led to severe humanitarian crises and widespread violence. Mali is plagued by insurgent groups, including those affiliated with Al-Qaeda, leading to ongoing violence and instability. Burkina Faso currently faces jihadist insurgencies in its northern and eastern regions, contributing to widespread displacement and humanitarian challenges.

In Somalia, the conflict involving the federal government and the Al-Qaeda-aligned extremist group Al-Shabaab continues to destabilize the country. The Democratic Republic of Congo is experiencing ongoing violence involving various armed groups, driven by ethnic tensions and regional power struggles. In the Central African Republic, political instability and clashes between government forces and rebel groups disrupt peace efforts and cause humanitarian crises.

Mozambique faces an Islamist insurgency that has led to significant violence, displacement, and economic disruption. Nigeria struggles with multiple conflicts, including the Boko Haram insurgency and clashes between farmers and herders and separatist movements. Libya remains divided with ongoing conflict between rival factions vying for control, and in Sudan ongoing conflicts in Darfur, South Kordofan, and the Blue Nile regions continue to cause significant displacement and suffering.

CONFLICT AT SCALE

I want to focus for a moment on Sudan. News coverage in Europe and the US focuses on war in Ukraine and Russia and in Israel and Gaza. Sudan is not mentioned. And yet, over 13,000 people are reported to have lost their lives since fighting began in April 2023.[11] Over 7 million people have been displaced.[12] And that's in just over a year. Half a million more are being displaced each month, yet the West does not hear about this war, or the other African conflicts.

[11] https://acleddata.com/conflict-watchlist-2024/sudan/

[12] https://reliefweb.int/report/sudan/sudan-humanitarian-update-4-january-2024-enar

Even discussing the scale of the conflict in Sudan can't express the scale and diversity of conflict across Africa. I listed ten countries with conflict, yet the RULAC (Rule of Law in Armed Conflicts), part of the Geneva Academy of International Humanitarian Law and Human Rights, lists thirty-five current conflicts in Africa.[13] Thirty-five.

War is indeed raging across Africa, so how could a unified defense system help? It is clear that a unified defense system could only exist once there is willingness to collaborate to bring about greater stability. Such a move would indeed take years or decades to bring about. But even though it seems hard right now, I want to advocate that it's worth fighting for. If leaders can collaborate to unite and protect, not only their own nations but other African nations, all of Africa becomes a more stable, richer place.

While many conflicts are internal and specific to African history, many are indeed influenced by external powers. While it may serve other nations for Africa to be at war with itself, it is up to Africa alone to end the bloodshed. A unified defense system would require significant investment, and I wonder how African nations are currently supported by other nations and whether that is what is holding Africa back from uniting on defense.

COLONIALISM: A FRENCH CASE STUDY

I want to take a deeper look at the symbiotic nature of foreign involvement in Africa and the impact that may have on defense by looking at Africa's relationship with France. France's relationship with Africa is deeply intertwined, both historically and economically, serving the interests of both regions. It is essential to understand that France's involvement in Africa is driven by self-interest rather than altruism. Historically, France has maintained long-standing ties with many African countries, especially its former colonies, and continues to wield influence politically, culturally, and economically.

---

[13] https://geneva-academy.ch/galleries/today-s-armed-conflicts

Economically, Africa is crucial to French interests. French companies have significant investments in sectors such as energy, mining, telecommunications, and agriculture in countries like Gabon, Côte d'Ivoire, and Senegal. The presence of over 40,000 French companies in Africa, including many multinational corporations, generates significant profits for French businesses and their investors. Furthermore, France relies on Africa for a substantial portion of its raw materials, including oil, gas, uranium, and minerals. Niger, for example, supplies a significant amount of the uranium used for France's nuclear energy program, which is crucial to the French energy sector.

It's fair to say the trade relationship between France and Africa supports jobs and economic growth in both regions, with France exporting machinery, vehicles, pharmaceuticals, and other goods to Africa while importing raw materials and agricultural products.

However, this relationship is becoming increasingly strained. In the Sahel region and elsewhere on the continent, people increasingly see France as a "diminished European power meddling in their nations' affairs."[14] They perceive France as importing natural resources, courting new unelected African leaders, and sometimes intervening with overbearing military force. This sentiment has intensified with recent military coups in West Africa, where French influence has waned. Guinea, Mali, Burkina Faso, and Niger are now ruled by generals who no longer wish to rely on France.

Many Africans believe that French troops are deployed primarily to ensure that French business interests remain uninterrupted. Local communities are widely reported to be deeply frustrated, as French promises to protect them from civil strife and terrorism have not been fulfilled. The security situation continues to deteriorate, and French soldiers are perceived negatively. In Niger, anti-French sentiments were evident during the military takeover, with demonstrators questioning France's

[14] https://www.dandc.eu/en/article/former-colonial-power-facing-deep-resentment-president-macrons-attempt-reset-relations-has

continued presence. They voiced their frustrations, asking why France remains when other former colonial powers left Africa decades ago.

Ongoing conflicts in African nations generally have negative repercussions for France and the broader international community. After all, conflicts disrupt economic stability and trade, affecting French businesses operating in Africa. Secure and stable environments are necessary for the continued operation and profitability of French investments in Africa, and wars can lead to the destruction of infrastructure, making business operations challenging.

Conflicts also lead to security concerns beyond the continent. Conflicts drive large numbers of refugees and migrants to seek safety and better opportunities elsewhere, including in France, which in turn creates socioeconomic and political challenges. Ultimately, France has a vested interest in regional stability to prevent the spread of terrorism and protect its strategic interests, including the security of its expatriates and military personnel, as well as trade, investment, and strategic partnerships.

France has traditionally supported African defense through various means, including military training and assistance, defense agreements, direct military intervention, and support for regional security initiatives. Extensive military training has been provided to numerous African countries, covering areas like tactics, counterterrorism, logistics, and peacekeeping operations. Additionally, France has conducted direct military interventions, such as Operation Barkhane in the Sahel region, although these efforts have been deemed unsuccessful by many.

The French example illustrates the symbiotic nature of the African–French relationship: Both France and Africa should benefit. However, when African nations perceive that France benefits too much, mistrust arises. The colonial legacy of these relationships leads to skepticism and a genuine sense that the French are not in it for purely benevolent reasons. Protecting French business activities and stemming terrorism are reasonable intentions, but mistrust leads to unrest, which in turn leads to more significant problems.

Anti-French feelings in Africa do not seem to affect views of other European countries or the US, which also has a long-standing military deployment in Niger. Increasingly, though, France is seen by many as a liability rather than an ally.

FOREIGN INVOLVEMENT

Of course, the alignment of African nations with superpowers in terms of defense is shaped by a complex web of historical ties and economic dependencies. African countries with historical ties to former colonial powers are often influenced in their defense alignments. For example, France maintains strong military relationships with its former colonies in West Africa, exemplified by military bases and ongoing counterterrorism operations in the Sahel region. The United Kingdom also retains defense links with countries including Kenya, Nigeria, and Ghana, offering military training and joint exercises.

The United States has strategic interests in Africa, primarily focused on countering terrorism and ensuring stability in key regions. Through the United States Africa Command (AFRICOM), the US engages in military cooperation, training, and support for African armies. The US has bases and military presence in countries such as Djibouti.

China's involvement in African defense is a growing phenomenon, marked by significant arms sales, military training, and peacekeeping contributions.[15] China's defense relationships often accompany broader economic investments under the Belt and Road Initiative. Beijing has established its first overseas military base in Djibouti, signaling its strategic interest in the region. Chinese military aid and technology are becoming more and more important to African nations, which is a worrying trend for Western powers, yet for many Africans less so.

Russia is reasserting its influence in Africa through defense cooperation, often providing military hardware and private military contractors. Russia's approach includes arms deals, military

[15] https://www.chathamhouse.org/2023/01/china-africa-relations

training, and agreements on defense cooperation with countries such as Sudan, the Central African Republic, and Mozambique. These relationships are partly driven by Russia's desire to counter Western influence in the region. And it's working.

The European Union engages with Africa on security through initiatives like the African Peace Facility, which supports African Union–led peacekeeping operations. NATO, while not deeply involved in Africa, has partnerships with the African Union and supports capacity-building efforts. But does foreign involvement in African defense protect Africa, or does it fuel tensions and support ongoing conflict?

ALTERNATIVE RELATIONSHIPS: RUSSIA

The problem with the downgrading of French involvement is that it leaves the door open for other countries, namely Russia. And Russia's involvement in Africa has boomed in recent years. While Russia offers an end to the lingering colonialism of French involvement, it simply creates a new form of colonialism in which African countries become further indebted to Russia.

Yet many Africans seem convinced and now hope that cooperation with China, Russia, or even the Gulf States might better serve their interests. Russian President Vladimir Putin is seen by some as a strong man supporting Africa's escape from postcolonial domination, despite this positioning being at odds with how the rest of the world sees him.

Russia has for years sent troops to Africa to support defense strategies and in the form of mercenaries. Just five years ago, few in the West would have heard of the Wagner Group, but now most people are aware of the group, and their former leader Yevgeny Prigozhin, after he attempted to march on Moscow, calling for the removal of the Russian defense minister. After this direct challenge to Putin, his days were numbered, and in August 2023 he was killed in a plane crash.

Wagner is well known, however, in Africa. Wagner has had a stronghold in Mali, after the country stopped relying on French troops. The security situation, though, did not improve, and the arrangement led to further instability and reported human rights abuses.

Russia's role in Africa is particularly concerning. After Prigozhin's death, Wagner was no more and instead assimilated into the Russian military and run as the "Russian Expeditionary Corps." While Wagner gave Russia some distance from what went on in Mali, the operation is now firmly under the control of the Russian government and fully out in the open. And in this more exposed state they are bolder than ever. They are said to offer African governments "regime survival packages" in exchange for access to strategically important natural resources.

Without French defense involvement, Russian mercenary forces have been allowed to walk in invited, and to an extent have been welcomed with open arms. Internal Russian documents exposed in a report by Jack Watling, land warfare specialist at the Royal United Services Institute (RUSI),[16] reveal efforts to change mining laws in West Africa, aiming to dislodge Western companies.

Under the control of Russian military intelligence, Wagner's African operations continue to thrive. They secure mineral rights from African nations in exchange for military support, providing regimes with the means to maintain power. In addition to Mali, this relationship is evident in countries like Libya, Burkina Faso, and the Central African Republic, where Wagner's presence bolsters ruling regimes. While providing immediate military advantages and economic benefits to their sponsors, the presence of mercenary groups like Wagner (and now simply Russian military) often prolongs conflicts, leads to significant human rights abuses, and undermines long-term stability and development.

WHY A UNIFIED DEFENSE SYSTEM DOESN'T EXIST TODAY

Today there are many reasons Africa does not have a unified defense system and why creating one would need Africa to embark on a long and hard journey. Diverse political landscapes,

[16] https://www.bbc.co.uk/news/world-africa-68322230

varying economic statuses, and historical rivalries hinder the collaborative efforts needed to establish such a system.

Sovereign policies and priorities have often stood in the way of deep military integration, and the logistical challenges of coordinating dozens of countries with different military capabilities and strategic doctrines are non-trivial. In addition, external powers—Russia as well as China and Gulf State involvement—now mean defense is well and truly established in a way that would stop Africa creating a unified policy and capability. Extracting foreign involvement and forging an independent path will be hard.

RETHINKING DEFENSE

Wars are no longer solely fought on the battlefield. While plenty of conflict in Africa is conventional armored warfare, we must not forget the role of cyber warfare in conflicts in Africa and elsewhere.

Cyber is increasingly a weapon for various actors in Africa, although it is perhaps less sophisticated and widespread compared to other regions like Europe or, specifically, Russia. African nations and non-state actors use cyber tactics to disrupt communication, spread propaganda, and influence public opinion. These tactics are often intended to destabilize governments, manipulate elections, and suppress opposition efforts. The tools used in African cyber warfare include social media manipulation, hacking into government websites, and disseminating disinformation to create chaos and mistrust.

On the other hand, cyber warfare in other parts of the world, such as the United States, Russia, and China, tends to be more advanced and integrated into broader military strategies. These nations employ highly sophisticated cyber capabilities to conduct espionage, sabotage critical infrastructure, and gain strategic advantages. Examples include Russia's alleged interference in the 2016 US presidential election, cyberattacks on Ukrainian power grids, and China's extensive cyber espionage campaigns targeting intellectual property and government secrets. The Chinese government has only recently been accused of hacking the UK's

Ministry of Defense and stealing personal details of members of the armed forces.[17]

While African cyber warfare efforts are growing, they often lack the technical sophistication and scale seen in conflicts involving major global powers. However, the impact can still be significant, as digital tools allow for rapid and widespread dissemination of misinformation and disruption of governmental functions, exacerbating existing tensions on the continent.

While Africa is less capable than other nations in terms of cyber protection, it is open to insidious attacks from perhaps unseen enemies. Yet the world is clear on which nations have the cyber capabilities to cause damage. The state actors' playbooks are well documented.

Russia's cyber warfare tactics are sophisticated and multifaceted, aimed at achieving strategic, military, and political objectives. The most well-known Russian cyberattack is the interference in the 2016 US presidential election. Russian operatives hacked into the Democratic National Committee and the email accounts of Democratic party officials, releasing stolen information to influence the election outcome. The "Internet Research Agency," a Russian troll farm, also conducted extensive social media campaigns to influence public opinion. Russia has repeatedly targeted Ukraine with cyberattacks. Russian hackers attacked Ukraine's power grid as early as 2015 and attacked Ukrainian government websites and financial systems in the run up to their invasion in 2022.

The NotPetya malware attack in 2017, which targeted Ukrainian companies, quickly spread globally, causing widespread disruption. The malware, widely believed to be created by Russian military intelligence, affected major corporations, including Maersk, Merck, and FedEx, resulting in billions of dollars in damages.

---

[17] https://www.politico.eu/article/suspected-china-hack-hits-uks-defense-ministry/

The 2018 Winter Olympics cyberattacks disrupted IT systems and attempted to discredit the International Olympic Committee following the ban on Russian athletes. Beyond Ukraine, Russian hackers have targeted critical infrastructure in the United States and Europe, including energy grids, water supply systems, and transportation networks. Such attacks often aim to gather intelligence.

Russia is well known for employing disinformation campaigns via social media platforms, spreading fake news and conspiracy theories with the intention of creating divisions within societies. This undermines trust in democratic institutions and exacerbates social and political tensions. These tactics reflect Russia's broader strategy of using cyber capabilities to achieve geopolitical objectives, influence global politics, and assert its power on the international stage. The sophistication and scale of these operations illustrate the significant threat posed by state-sponsored cyber warfare.

While we may think Russia and others are only involved in providing conventional defense to African nations, just think of the power they hold and could deploy through cyber warfare. Influencing elections, creating social unrest, and destabilizing nations can all be done without any troops, tanks, or missiles.

INCREASING DEFENSE SPENDING

Look at defense spending in comparison with other nations. Countries like Algeria, Egypt, and South Africa are among the top spenders on defense in Africa, although this is not necessarily reflected in defense spending as a percentage of GDP—where GDP is large. As an example, Mali spends 2.8 percent but is very reliant on defense support from foreign powers.

Algeria: 5.6 percent
Chad: 3.2 percent
Democratic Republic of Congo: 1.0 percent
Egypt: 2.5 percent
Ethiopia: 0.6 percent
Ghana: 0.7 percent

Kenya: 1.2 percent
Mali: 2.8 percent
Morocco: 3.5 percent
Nigeria: 0.5 percent
South Africa: 1.0 percent
Sudan: 2.3 percent

This shows a patchy picture across Africa. African countries with large expenditures ensure they maintain robust armed forces, equipped with relatively modern technology compared to other African nations. This military might allows them to play pivotal roles in regional security matters. These countries could lead the charge in bolstering defense spending, securing against foreign defense involvement, and moving toward a united African defense strategy.

When looking at non-African countries, we also see huge disparity in defense spending as a percentage of GDP, but it is clear that countries that are focused on defense are investing heavily:

United States: 3.5 percent
United Kingdom: 2.3 percent
France: 1.8 percent
Germany 1.2 percent
China: 1.7 percent
Israel: 5.0 percent
Russia: 4.0 percent
Ukraine: 4.0 percent

MOVES TOWARD SUCH A SYSTEM

Regional cooperation has been developing. African nations are increasingly cooperating on defense through regional organizations such as the African Union and bodies like the Economic Community of West African States. The African Union has made progress with its African Peace and Security Architecture, aiming to promote peace, security, and stability.

The AU's African Standby Force is an initiative aimed at enhancing the continent's ability to respond to crises independently. The African Standby Force is an international, continental

African, and multidisciplinary peacekeeping force with military, police, and civilian contingents that act under the direction of the African Union. The ASF is to be deployed in times of crisis in Africa. This is currently the closest thing Africa has to a central defense strategy.

THE ROLE OF THE PUBLIC SECTOR

Imagine for a moment that a group of African nations commits to leading the move to an African defense system without external influence. A core group of public sector leaders would need to lead that charge. It would take political might and skill and significant nerve to hold strong in the face of the huge influence from the likes of Russia.

Implementing a standardized system across such a diverse continent is clearly not going to be easy. In addition to the fact that many countries rely on assistance from outside, other challenges include differences in language, policies, and levels of technological advancement. And that's if you can convince African leaders that they won't lose their individual sovereignty by committing to a continent-wide military alliance.

THE ROLE OF TECHNOLOGY: CYBER IS THE KEY TO AFRICAN DEFENSE

For Africa to enjoy stability supported by a unified defense system, it must increase its capability in cybersecurity. Africa needs to develop the expertise in cybersecurity equal to that of Russia or China. There is no reason, after all, that these skills and capabilities could not be developed. In line with my vision for better education across Africa, skills need to be developed to help Africa compete globally and to protect itself locally.

I would go so far as to say that cyber skills should be central to an African defense strategy and central to helping wean African nations off support from foreign powers. Cyber capabilities go hand in hand with intelligence capabilities. By focusing on these aspects of defense, Africa can better protect itself.

DEFENSE TECHNOLOGY NEEDS INVESTMENT

The broader defense technology ecosystem is interesting and encouraging. There are already established defense technology industries with successful players in countries including South Africa, Egypt, and Nigeria. The start-up ecosystem of smaller innovators in defense technology in Africa is also gradually evolving. Several factors are contributing to the development of this ecosystem, including increasing investments, governmental support, and collaboration with international partners.

South Africa is at the forefront of defense technology innovation in Africa with a relatively mature defense industry and a number of start-ups emerging in the fields of cybersecurity, unmanned systems, and advanced manufacturing. Companies like Aerosud and Paramount Group foster innovation through partnerships and incubator programs.

In Nigeria, the focus on counterterrorism and internal security has spurred interest in defense technology solutions. Start-ups in Nigeria are increasingly exploring areas such as drone technology, surveillance systems, and cybersecurity.

Kenya has also seen a rise in defense technology start-ups, particularly in the cybersecurity sector. The country's burgeoning technology scene, centered around Nairobi's Silicon Savannah, is producing innovative solutions tailored to local security needs. Start-ups like Cyborg Systems are developing advanced cybersecurity solutions, while others are focusing on surveillance and data analytics to support defense and security operations.

Companies in Morocco are developing technologies related to surveillance, border security, and cybersecurity, addressing both national security needs and broader regional challenges. Egypt is also investing heavily in the space.

However, funding remains a significant hurdle, as defense technology requires substantial capital investment. While there is growing interest from private investors and venture capital firms, many start-ups still struggle to secure the necessary funding to scale.

COULD SPACE TECHNOLOGY BE THE KEY?

Much of defense technology innovation is far from traditional; indeed, it offers significant innovation. Yet I wonder if Africa might not do better by leapfrogging the natural next step of defense technology and look directly to space technology. At the very least, these two areas should be developed hand in hand. Space technology and defense technology are increasingly intertwined, with advancements in one often driving innovations in the other, after all.

My 2050 vision of an Africa protected by a network of satellites is not so farfetched. Indeed, there are already companies working on this. "The African space economy is projected to grow by 16.16 percent to USD 22.64 billion by 2026" according to the African Space Industry Annual Report.[18]

Satellites provide real-time surveillance and reconnaissance capabilities, allowing for the monitoring of borders, tracking of military movements, and identification of potential threats. For African nations, this means enhanced capability to protect their territories, manage conflicts, and ensure national security.

Space-based communication systems are vital for defense operations too. They provide secure and reliable communication channels that are less susceptible to disruption than ground-based systems. In Africa, terrestrial communication infrastructure can be limited or vulnerable, so satellite communication can ensure that military and emergency services can coordinate effectively. Satellites are also crucial for environmental monitoring. For Africa, investing in space technology can stimulate innovation, create high-tech jobs, and build a skilled workforce capable of driving future technological progress as well as shoring up defense.

---

[18] https://spaceinafrica.com/2023/08/28/african-space-industry-annual-report-2023-edition/

OVERCOMING THE CHALLENGES

Overcoming these varied challenges requires a multipronged approach. First, there are some practical strategies that could be employed. Building trust among African nations through increased diplomatic engagements and joint military exercises could lay the groundwork for deeper cooperation. Starting small on less critical areas would be where I'd start. Simple things like implementing standardized training programs and defense protocols could alleviate concerns about uneven military capabilities. Then, of course, establishing clear legal frameworks could address concerns about sovereignty and control.

Technology transfer agreements and collaborative defense projects could be promoted to level the technological playing field across the continent. By investing in local defense industries and encouraging regional defense collaboration, Africa could reduce its dependence on external military suppliers and build its own sustainable and innovative defense capabilities.

But these are just simple practical strategies that move the needle to improving the status quo rather than rethinking defense "root and branch." I think it needs way more than this; the concept of defense itself needs to be reimagined.

MOVING FORWARD

While the vision of a unified African defense system presents numerous challenges, early efforts at collaboration could eventually lead to a more secure, cooperative, and independent African continent. By continuing to build on regional partnerships, and by investing in technology alongside conventional defense tactics, Africa can move closer to a standardized defense capability.

Standardized, in my mind, means strong, and as such, a handful of African countries will need to take a lead on such initiatives with less involvement from others, to begin with at least. Not all African countries will be able to collaborate or participate from day one, so the effort needs to be led by those who can muster support, shore up existing capability, and invest in new defensive capabilities. Membership of a standardized defense union may be contingent on nations meeting certain criteria. Initially, a group of nations who are not in conflict, who have resources to invest, and can commit to technology-enabled defense should lead the way. Private companies should also be supported to create the new wave of technology to support Africa in its defense ambition, and leaders must cede some control to the private sector and create partnerships that foster innovation.

DEFENSE-CENTRIC MINDSET SHIFT

The required mindset, when it comes to defense, is, of course, one of strength, courage, and innovation. The political will for Africa to unite must be greater than the will for individual nations to align with external powers. A key risk area is that African leaders are wooed by foreign superpowers and private companies offering benefits today at the expense of stability tomorrow.

Indeed, Dr. Alex Vines suggests, "Managing how to promote national, regional and continental priorities with the growing number of foreign suitors will require African states to prioritize better and could result in having to make difficult choices, more often."[19]

Next up, after taking the difficult choice not to get into bed with potential state actors, African leaders need to bolster the skills that really matter; those skills are not conventional military skills alone. Investment must be made in cyber capabilities, and to support that, investment must be made in technology education and infrastructure.

An ambitious vision is required to understand the traditional approach to defense will keep Africa controlled by those who can think bigger. Another key risk, therefore, is that leaders think too small and too near term. Africa must future-proof its defense with defense and space technology starting today.

I want to see African cyber capabilities, defense technology, and space technology grow to level the playing field. For me,

---

[19] https://www.chathamhouse.org/2024/01/whats-stake-africa-2024

therefore, this is as much about investment in a homegrown African defense industry and technology as it is about troops and training. We need a holistic approach that matches human capital with technology, innovation, and investment. We also need venture and private equity investment in African defense and space technology.

IMAGINE 2050 WITH A UNIFIED DEFENSE SYSTEM

Imagine, if you will, the African skies monitored by a network of satellites designed and launched by an African space agency, built on the continent's technological prowess. On the ground, peace-keeping missions are coordinated and effective, addressing conflicts with a swift and unified response that reflects a continent-wide commitment to peace and stability. African citizens, once living under the omnipresent fear of cross-border and local insurgencies, now enjoy a greater sense of security.

I believe security contributes to a flourishing economy, allowing all Africans to enjoy a greater sense of opportunity and prosperity. This 2050 vision seems a long way off, and much would have to be done for it to pass. However, I believe it is possible, so here I outline strategies for achieving it.

Chapter 9

WHAT IF AFRICA HAD A STANDARDIZED EDUCATION SYSTEM THAT NURTURED FUTURE LEADERS?

My first what if is about education. It is big and it is bold. I want to imagine a world in which all Africans have access to good quality education, from early years to higher or further education. From my perspective, with a background deeply rooted in problem solving and a keen focus on innovation, education is fundamentally central to development for several reasons.

First, education empowers individuals by equipping them with knowledge and skills, enabling them to fully participate in their economies and societies. This empowerment is crucial for fostering a sense of agency and self-efficacy, which in turn drives personal and community development. Moreover, education serves as a critical driver of economic growth and innovation. By providing people with the skills needed to navigate and succeed in a rapidly changing global marketplace, education fuels the development of new technologies and business models that boost economic productivity and competitiveness. Education also contributes to social stability and effective governance by promoting critical thinking and a deeper understanding of civic responsibilities.

WHY EDUCATION?

My interest in how societies function and the role of leadership with a small "l" highlight how education can cultivate informed citizens capable of making thoughtful decisions about their leaders and government policies. I am a staunch advocate for policies and practices that lead to more equitable outcomes, and I see education as a powerful tool for achieving equity and inclusion. It provides opportunities for all individuals, regardless of their background, to improve their life circumstances. It creates fair and inclusive workplaces and societies.

I also recognize that for Africa, or any region, to be competitive on a global scale, a well-educated workforce is crucial. This is not just about basic education, but also about higher education and continuous professional development that keeps pace with global standards and advancements in technology.

Education is a critical infrastructure component. It is central to creating the environments that foster innovation, equity, and leadership, which are necessary for development in an increasingly complex world.

WHY THIS DOESN'T EXIST TODAY

We see some green shoots of this vision today, including the increase in African start-ups and more Africans taking up higher education. It is estimated that in Nigeria alone there will be another 50 million young people in education over the age of fifteen by 2050.[20]

However, we need to look at why Africa isn't on par with even some of the lesser developed European nations. Today, Africa's education systems vary significantly across the continent, with disparities in quality and access. Many schools lack resources and are not equipped to provide education beyond basic literacy and numeracy. Current curricula often do not include components that foster leadership qualities, and there is a significant

[20] https://www.timeshighereducation.com/depth/how-can-africas-vast-appetite-higher-education-be-met

gap in teacher training and educational infrastructure to support such an ambitious transformation.

Africa's education system faces host of challenges. Underfunding is a critical issue in many African countries, as limited budgets lead to insufficient classroom spaces, lack of teaching materials, and poorly paid and inadequately trained teachers. This financial strain hinders the overall quality of education provided to students.

Access to education is also a significant hurdle. Geographical barriers, economic hardship, and persistent social issues such as gender biases restrict many children's ability to attend school. In rural areas, the problem is exacerbated as children may have to travel long distances to reach the nearest school, which can decrease attendance rates and increase dropout rates.

The quality of education in many parts of Africa suffers due to these funding and access issues. Classrooms are often overcrowded, and there is a lack of individual attention available to students. This environment contributes to low literacy and numeracy levels among graduates, posing further challenges to their future opportunities and the ability to contribute effectively to their communities.

Dropout rates are particularly high, especially among girls, and are driven by socioeconomic pressures and cultural expectations that prioritize early marriage or labor over continuing education. These challenges hinder the potential for many young people across the continent to achieve personal growth and contribute to the development of their countries.

However, it is important to say that what hinders a young person in one country may be very different from what hinders a young person in another country. It's a patchy picture, and that is why I am advocating for an African wide approach.

THE PATCHY PICTURE

The disparity in education quality and access across Africa is significant, with countries like Seychelles setting positive examples of what can be achieved with proper investment and policies.

In contrast, nations like Chad and CAR illustrate the severe impacts of conflict and underfunding of education systems. Any efforts to improve educational access and quality across Africa must consider these diverse conditions and tailor approaches to meet specific local needs and challenges.

By way of comparison, let's look at education spend as a percentage of GDP[21] both in and outside of Africa:

- Cuba spends 11.5 percent of GDP on education.
- Germany spends 8.85 percent of GDP on education.
- Namibia spends 9.4 percent of GDP on education.
- The United Kingdom spends 5.3 percent of GDP on education.
- The European Union spends 5 percent of GDP on education.
- Sub-Saharan Africa spends 3.2 percent of GDP on education.
- Ghana spends 2.9 percent of GDP on education.
- Sudan spends 2 percent GDP on education.

The patchy picture across Africa impacts people across the wealth spectrum. While lower-income people may struggle to access education, richer people are looking elsewhere to fill the gap.

AFRICAN COUNTRIES WITH THE BEST EDUCATION SYSTEMS

The Seychelles holds the highest ranking for education in Africa, largely due to its government's investment in education, which amounts to approximately 10 percent of its GDP. The small island nation has achieved near-universal literacy and has schools equipped with relatively modern facilities and technologies.

Mauritius also ranks high in terms of educational quality in Africa. The government provides free education from the pre-primary level up to the tertiary level, a rarity in Africa. The country has a well-structured educational framework and significant investment in educational technology.

[21] https://data.worldbank.org/indicator/SE.XPD.TOTL.GD.ZS

While South Africa faces challenges regarding inequality, it still boasts some of the continent's best universities and a robust higher education system. Efforts to improve primary and secondary education quality continue, focusing on reducing disparities influenced by the apartheid era.

AFRICAN COUNTRIES WITH THE WORST EDUCATION SYSTEMS

Chad suffers from one of the weakest education systems in Africa and has one of the world's lowest literacy rates. Factors such as extreme poverty, political instability, and cultural practices hinder the development of education. School attendance is very low, and gender disparities are significant, with many girls not receiving any formal education.

CAR has an educational system severely impacted by ongoing conflicts and economic crises. Infrastructure is lacking, and many children are more likely to be involved in labor than in the classroom. Educational facilities are often used as shelters or bases during conflicts, further disrupting access to education.

Eritrea faces critical challenges in its education sector, including government policies that sometimes interfere with access to education. The country has strict control over educational institutions, and there are significant issues regarding academic freedom and accessibility.

THE SKILLS FARM: WORKFORCE DEVELOPMENT AT SCALE

Much of my work is about solving problems through innovation. While my vision for African education borrows a lot from the successes of North American and European education systems, I also believe Africans should determine education on their own terms. Why should it take three to five years to complete a degree? Why should you be indebted to a student loan for decades? Why, in our connected world, can't we bring global teachers to Africa and develop and retain our talent? How can we innovate skills training programs so that they deliver more relevant skills faster?

I have an idea for a new way to learn skills and earn qualifications. I call it the Skills Farm. It is home grown, organic, and possible anywhere, and it is innovative and rapid. I am borrowing from the concept of the business accelerator and the mini-MBA. I want to do away with the idea that it must take three to five years to earn a degree. What if it could take one? What if that degree was supported by worldclass tutors? What if that degree was funded by a corporate sponsor who then guaranteed you a job upon completion?

Imagine higher education "accelerators," if you will: intensive, fast-paced programs designed to provide students with the essential knowledge and skills typically gained through traditional degree programs but in a much shorter time frame. Similar to mini-MBAs, these accelerated qualifications aim to efficiently equip students with practical, industry-relevant education and work experience. The concept combines academic learning with hands-on experience in an industry setting, enabling students to quickly transition from education to employment. These programs would allow students to complete their education in a fraction of the time it would take to earn a traditional degree, which is particularly beneficial for individuals seeking to enter the workforce quickly or for those looking to switch careers.

Accelerated programs are often less expensive than traditional degree programs due to their shorter duration, making higher education more accessible to a broader range of students, including those who may not have the financial resources for longer courses. Collaborations with industries ensure that the curriculum is relevant and up to date with current market needs. These partnerships can also provide students with networking opportunities, internships, and job placements upon completion. The curriculum is highly focused on the most relevant aspects of study, allowing students to concentrate on what is most important for their career goals. These could be set up in partnership by universities and businesses to a unified standard, all designed to keep skilled workers and leaders in Africa for the long term.

And I don't believe the skills farm concept should be limited to the sort of skills associated with university study. I want all Africans to benefit from new intense training opportunities. Blue-collar workers could also be rapidly trained through these skills farms. Imagine that the African manufacturing sector is a key strategic focus; various nations intend to expand their manufacturing output. African workers could be rapidly trained in the skills required, not only to deliver the manufacturing capability historically associated with China—the manufacture of cheap basic products—but could also be trained in more advanced techniques required to compete with China in light of its ambition to develop more self-sufficient technology manufacturing capabilities.

The skills farm concept of shortening the time it takes to gain relevant employable skills could apply across Africa's industrial diversification. There'd be courses that prepared workers for careers in manufacturing, technology, infrastructure development, the renewable energy sector, the blue economy, travel and tourism, and more.

IMPACT

By investing in the minds of its young people today, Africa can secure a brighter, more prosperous future. A standardized education system that nurtures future leaders could dramatically reshape Africa's future by fostering enhanced governance, economic innovation, social cohesion, and global influence. Free access to education would radically accelerate development across the continent. Indeed, without better education, other initiatives may fail. Education, in my opinion, is key to growth, period.

The potential benefit of a standardized African education system is immense. But more vitally, on a personal level, such a system would ensure every child in Africa is allowed to reach their potential.

FUNDING AN INCREASED INVESTMENT IN AFRICAN EDUCATION

To grasp why free education cannot currently be universally provided across Africa and why the quality of education often lags behind that found in the US, UK, and Europe, let's first examine the tax revenues in these regions. Developed nations such as the UK, US, and Germany boast substantial proportions of their working-age populations contributing to national tax revenues: 75 percent, 66 percent, and 47.5 percent respectively. This tax base allows these countries to fund public services extensively, including free or heavily subsidized education systems.

In the African countries of Nigeria and Ghana, on the other hand, the tax-paying figures are starkly lower, with 1.7 percent each. Such low tax participation severely restricts African nations' abilities to generate the funds necessary for widespread public services, including education. South Africa is perhaps an outlier with 18 percent. The disparity in tax intake is primarily due to larger informal economies in Africa where many transactions escape the formal tax system, high rates of unemployment and underemployment reducing the number of people eligible to pay taxes, and challenges such as tax evasion and inadequate tax collection systems.

The limited fiscal capacity means that governments in countries like Nigeria and Ghana are constrained in their ability to fund education comprehensively. This results in underfunded schools, lack of teaching materials, and inadequate educational infrastructure, often forcing families to pay toward their children's education.

Formalizing the informal sector could significantly widen the tax base, while enhancing the efficiency and transparency of tax collection mechanisms can increase public trust and compliance, thus raising revenues. Leveraging international investments can also help bridge temporary funding gaps as long-term domestic capacities are developed. Additionally, engaging the private sector in education through public–private partnerships can introduce more resources and innovation into the public education system.

Tackling the issue of funding education in Africa requires a comprehensive approach that considers economic, administrative, and social dimensions to effectively increase the tax base and support sustainable investment in quality education for all. Implementing a continent-wide standardized education system in Africa, particularly one focused on leadership, faces several significant challenges. African countries vary widely in their current state of educational policies, resources, and national priorities, making it complex to align them into a cohesive, unified system. Each country has developed its educational framework based on its unique historical, economic, and social contexts, which would need to be considered.

The resource allocation required to implement such a system is substantial. There would need to be a significant investment to upgrade existing school infrastructures, train and possibly retrain teachers, and develop curricula that can effectively nurture leadership qualities across diverse populations. The financial burden would of course be challenging for many African nations, particularly those with limited budgets and other pressing socioeconomic needs.

To overcome barriers, there's a lot of work to do and many factors need to happen in unison. My first focus would be significant investment in teacher training by attracting and nurturing public–private partnerships.

HOW THE PRIVATE SECTOR COULD KEEP SKILLED WORKERS IN AFRICA

The model of subsidized education linked to a commitment to serve in a specific sector or region presents a valuable blueprint that can be adapted to the corporate world, especially in the context of African development. This approach could be particularly transformative when integrated into public–private partnerships, whereby corporations play a pivotal role in sponsoring education for African students.

In this model, corporations would sponsor the education of students in critical fields that align with their organizational needs, such as technology, engineering, health care, and management, with the agreement that these students would work for the sponsoring company for a minimum period upon graduation. This strategy would not only help students by reducing or eliminating the financial barriers to obtaining advanced education but would also benefit corporations by ensuring access to a steady flow of skilled workers trained in relevant disciplines.

Corporations that engage in sponsoring educational programs could create a tailored pipeline of skilled labor to meet their specific needs, reduce recruitment costs and turnover rates, and enhance workforce stability and expertise. By actively shaping educational programs, corporations ensure that training aligns closely with industry standards and anticipated future technological advancements. Such alignment would facilitate a smoother and more efficient transition from education to employment for graduates.

This model could play a crucial role in the broader economic development of the region. By boosting employment rates and cultivating a more skilled workforce, businesses would attract further investment and enhance the overall economic landscape. Corporations would also improve their community engagement and corporate social responsibility profiles. Also, on a more local level, by investing in local education, they build stronger relationships with local communities and governments, establishing a foundation of trust.

For such a model to be effective, robust partnerships between educational institutions, corporations, and governments are essential. Stakeholders must collaborate to design educational programs that not only meet the skill requirements of the corporations but also ensure that the educational standards are high and that programs provide real, long-term value to students beyond the tenure of their obligation to the sponsoring entity.

It's crucial to ensure such arrangements are ethical and genuinely benefit the students. Students should receive fair compensation and working conditions, consistent with market standards, to prevent exploitation.

Corporate-sponsored education could become a cornerstone of sustainable economic development strategy in Africa, helping bridge the gap between education and employment and fostering a new generation of skilled professionals ready to contribute to their countries' growth and prosperity.

THE BRAIN DRAIN

A key problem is that so many Africans leave Africa. The fantastic African diaspora that is celebrated everywhere else really is a problem for Africa. Indeed, my parents left Africa and chose to bring me up in Europe instead. They felt the entire family would be better elsewhere. I find this particularly sad; they escaped very real struggles in Africa to a perhaps more prosperous Austria. While other countries offer more peace and stability, better opportunities for education and work, many will seek to make that journey and leave their homeland behind. How can we encourage people to stay, to develop their talents at home and use them for the greater good of Africa, not for Europe, the US, or elsewhere?

My parents' story was one of escaping poverty. They were not wealthy when they chose to leave Africa; they went, as they saw it at the time, "out of necessity." But for others, it is nowadays far easier to leave. First let's look at the allure of elsewhere for wealthy Africans. In our global economy, many wealthy Africans choose to send their children overseas for their education due to a combination of the limitations of local educational systems and the perceived advantages of international schooling. Overseas schools, particularly in North America and Europe, are renowned for their high educational standards, rigorous academic programs, and broader range of subjects. Overseas schools often boast better resources, including well-stocked libraries, state-of-the-art laboratories, and experienced teaching staff, which can provide a richer learning environment than those available in many African countries.

Degrees from prestigious universities abroad are highly regarded globally, offering a competitive edge in the global job market. For wealthy African families, there is also a social prestige associated with foreign education, viewing the ability to send children abroad as a status symbol and demonstration of their genuine success and/or in many cases success through corruption.

Studying abroad exposes students to international networks, potentially leading to better career opportunities both internationally and within their home countries. These networks can be crucial for future business opportunities and career advancement. Furthermore, countries that host international students typically offer more structured career paths and higher employment rates in skilled professions, presenting graduates with robust job prospects.

Beyond academic and career benefits, studying abroad allows students to experience different cultures, which can broaden their perspectives and enhance personal development. This exposure is invaluable for personal growth and understanding global issues. Additionally, immersion in a new culture is an excellent opportunity for language acquisition, appealing to students looking to enhance their multilingual skills.

In regions of Africa experiencing political turmoil, economic instability, or high rates of crime, families may send their children abroad as a way to ensure their safety and provide them with a more stable environment in which to study. Subjects like advanced medical research, aerospace engineering, and certain fine arts are often better established in universities abroad. Research opportunities, particularly at the postgraduate level, are more abundant in universities that are well funded and equipped with the necessary facilities and expert mentors.

I find the aspiration to educate one's children somewhere else to be depressing. On a personal level, I am all for personal choice and freedoms; if someone wants to choose education from elsewhere that is up to them, but collectively, the fact that so many choose education elsewhere means that we have a problem but a problem we can fix.

There is clearly a need for African nations to enhance their own educational systems and ensure that high-quality education is accessible to more of its citizens. If the wealthy seek private education elsewhere, is there not a gap in the market for high-quality education within Africa? Afterall, many of Europe's top independent schools have spotted such a gap in the market in Asia and are launching their own branded outposts in Malaysia, Singapore, Thailand and China—so why not Africa?

At the university level too, it is vital we develop new strategies to encourage those with talent and skills to stay. Austria once considered a policy that provided free or low-cost training to medical students under the condition that they practice medicine within the country for at least five years after completing their education. Sadly, the policy didn't make it into practice, but I really like the idea. The approach was designed to ensure that the investment in health care education benefits the local health care system directly, addressing potential shortages and ensuring that the community has adequate medical coverage.

One of the main advantages would have been to encourage students to pursue medical careers by reducing the financial barriers associated with medical education. As medical training can be exceedingly expensive, subsidized education removes a significant hurdle, making the profession more accessible to a broader demographic. Additionally, by requiring graduates to work in the country for a set period, the policy helps to maintain a steady supply of health care professionals. While this didn't come to pass in Austria, it's still a concept we can learn from, and one we see elsewhere.

Similar policies are found in other sectors and countries, particularly in education. For example, some regions offer scholarships or loan forgiveness to teachers who agree to serve in high-need areas or in specific subjects for a certain number of years. These programs aim to attract teachers in areas that have acute shortages, such as in STEM education or special education, or to underserved geographical areas. What I find so disruptive about this concept is that it not only guarantees you a relevant education, but also a job.

Post-education, Africa really needs to focus on talent retention in the workplace—in all sectors and at all levels. We can't build better education systems only to see more and more of Africa's youth disappear around the world. We need African talent to remain in Africa.

IMAGINE 2050, WHEN EVERY CHILD HAS ACCESS TO A ROBUST EDUCATION

Imagine a future when every child in Africa has access to a standardized and free education system from their early years all the way through higher or further education. The educational framework is focused on cultivating prosperity and has the potential to develop leadership qualities, critical thinking, and civic responsibility from a young age.

Imagine that by the year 2050 Africa has redefined itself as an education powerhouse. Schools and universities across the continent operate under a unified curriculum that emphasizes leadership development, ethical governance, and social entrepreneurship. Educational institutions are not just centers of learning; they are incubators for the world's next wave of innovators and thought leaders.

Robust educational access is made possible through public–private partnerships that ensure education is freely accessible to all, regardless of economic background. Governments across African nations have prioritized education, implementing policies that fund schools and universities through a combination of public funds, increased taxes, international grants, and partnerships with the private sector. Strategic collaborations have resulted in the establishment of state-of-the-art educational facilities equipped with the latest technology and learning tools. Teachers are valued and well paid and choose to remain in Africa to develop their careers. Furthermore, African schools and universities attract some of the best teaching talent globally to bolster their already dynamic skills.

From the onset of their educational journey, children in Africa benefit from free access to pre-primary education, setting a strong foundation in literacy, numeracy, and critical thinking skills. As they progress to primary and secondary levels, the curriculum expands to include advanced science, technology, engineering, arts, and mathematics (STEAM) education, alongside courses in ethics, leadership, and, importantly, civic responsibility—a broad and inclusive educational approach ensures that students are not only academically proficient but also well-rounded individuals prepared to lead and innovate.

The impact of educational reforms is profound and far reaching. Young people in Africa grow to become highly ambitious, motivated to address the challenges facing their communities, countries, and the continent at large. They are not waiting for opportunities; they are creating them, leading grassroots initiatives, starting companies, and advocating for sustainable practices and policies.

Higher education and further education institutions continue this trajectory, offering specialized programs that align closely with industry needs and global trends. These institutions maintain strong partnerships with global universities and corporations, providing students with internships and research opportunities that further their practical experience and global perspective.

The ripple effect of this expansive educational access is evident in the economy, which sees a surge in innovation and entrepreneurship. Graduates, equipped with world-class education and leadership skills, are entering the workforce ready to contribute meaningfully. They are starting businesses that solve real-world problems, leveraging technology to create sustainable solutions and entering politics to advocate for progressive policies.

By 2050, the vision of a universally educated and empowered African youth will become a reality, setting a precedent for what is possible when nations invest wholeheartedly in the potential of their young people. Africa's place on the world stage is not only as participant but as a leader, reshaping global dynamics through the strength and vision of its educated youth. This scenario is not just a dream but a tangible future that could be brought about with a commitment to education by government and corporate leaders of today.

Chapter 10

WHAT IF AFRICA HAD A UNIFIED HEALTH CARE SYSTEM ACCESSIBLE TO ALL?

Improved health care outcomes are important for all of us as individuals, but also for nation-states. For Africa at large. Good health contributes to broader social and political stability; healthy populations are more productive, economically stable, and less likely to experience social unrest. By investing in a unified health care system, African nations can foster a more stable and prosperous continent, creating a virtuous cycle of health and development. Health is indeed wealth, for individuals and for Africa.

THE DOCTOR'S OFFICE ISN'T FOR EVERYONE

Of course, low-cost accessible health care for all Africans sounds like a good idea, right? Well, not to everyone. As an aside, I met a man in March of 2024 on a trip to Ghana who had never visited a dentist and rarely visited a doctor. Some readers might imagine a person with bad teeth and ill health, but I assure you, this couldn't be further from the truth. The man, in his fifties, was healthy and happy. As we chatted, he said he couldn't imagine why he'd want to visit a doctor or dentist, and he certainly didn't want to get into the habit of it. Of course, this man was lucky—lucky not to have suffered serious disease. Had he suffered serious disease I am sure he may have found his way to appropriate health care. But his point to me was this: "Where I live, with my lifestyle, supported by my community, I don't need (advanced) health care. I live a healthy lifestyle so I have health." It struck me that living a more Western way of life and eating processed foods would be what might rob this man of his health and cause him then to need more advanced health care.

Of course, not all Africans are so lucky. Many need health care: Children need health care, women need health care, the elderly need health care. We need to prevent diseases and ensure healthy lifestyles are lived by all. But he had a point; for him, the fact that he didn't need health care was a point of pride, and he saw Western style development as a cause of disease and suffering. For him, traditional remedies worked best and kept him well.

THE CURRENT STATE OF HEALTH CARE ACROSS AFRICA

Today, the state of health care in Africa is patchy, as access and quality vary widely from one region to another. In many countries, health care systems are underfunded, understaffed, and overwhelmed by the burden of both communicable and non-communicable diseases. The contrast between nations is stark. Some countries have made significant strides in improving health care, while others continue to struggle with basic health infrastructure and services.

HEALTH DISPARITIES

There is a clear divide between the highest and lowest spenders. Countries like South Africa, Botswana, and Namibia allocate substantial portions of their GDP to health care. South Africa, for instance, spends between 8 and 9 percent of its GDP on health care,[22] striving to provide universal health coverage.

[22] https://corporateandinvestment.standardbank.com/cib/global/insights/how-is-healthcare-activity-in-south-africa-measured

On the other end of the spectrum, countries like the Central African Republic, South Sudan, and Chad invest far less. These nations often spend less than 2 percent of their GDP on health, resulting in poor outcomes for citizens. The health care systems in these countries are characterized by shortages of doctors and nurses, inadequate facilities, and limited access to essential medicines and technologies.

In countries with minimal health care investment, the impact on citizens is profound. High maternal and infant mortality rates, low life expectancy, and the prevalence of preventable diseases paint a grim picture. For example, in the Central African Republic, life expectancy is just over fifty years, and access to basic health services is limited to urban areas, leaving rural populations underserved. The lack of investment means that diseases such as malaria, tuberculosis, and HIV/AIDS thrive, with insufficient resources to combat them effectively.

AFRICAN COUNTRIES WITH ADVANCED HEALTH SYSTEMS

Of course, there is plenty of advanced health care in Africa. Countries such as South Africa, Rwanda, and Ghana have taken significant steps to develop truly advanced health systems. South Africa's health infrastructure includes a mix of public and private services, extensive hospital networks, and advanced medical training institutions. Rwanda, known for its innovative approaches, has implemented community-based health insurance schemes that have dramatically increased health care access and use. Ghana's national health insurance scheme aims to provide affordable health care to all citizens, with a focus on reducing out-of-pocket expenses. But there's more to be done.

RETHINKING HEALTH CARE: IS A UNIFIED SYSTEM THE ANSWER?

I believe a unified health care system in Africa is likely to bring better health care to all Africans for several reasons. Centralized coordination, economies of scale, resource pooling, standardized care, and improved accessibility are just few of the benefits such a system could offer.

Centralized coordination and management would allow for more efficient handling of health care policies, resources, and initiatives. Distribution of medical supplies and health care professionals and the implementation of health programs can be managed more effectively. With centralized management, resources can be directed where they are most needed, addressing gaps in the system.

By operating on a larger, continental scale, a unified system can benefit from economies of scale. Bulk purchasing of medications, medical equipment, and supplies would lower costs, making health care more affordable. Financial efficiency could translate into greater investments in health care infrastructure, more affordable services for patients, and the ability to provide a wider range of treatments and preventive care.

Pooling resources across countries allows for better utilization of health care assets. Specialized medical facilities and expertise can be shared among neighboring countries, ensuring that patients have access to high-quality care without needing to travel long distances. Resource pooling can also extend to health care research and development, leading to advancements in medical treatments and public health initiatives.

Standardized care would be another benefit. Establishing common protocols for disease prevention, diagnosis, and treatment can lead to more consistent and higher-quality care.

A unified system can address the disparity in access to services between urban and rural areas by ensuring health care infrastructure is evenly developed and remote areas are not neglected. Mobile clinics, telemedicine, and decentralized health centers can be more effectively implemented, improving access for those in remote areas.

A unified system would facilitate comprehensive data collection and analysis on health trends, disease outbreaks, and health care outcomes. Data saves lives and is crucial to informed decision making. With a better understanding of health challenges, governments and health organizations can respond more effectively to public health crises and long-term health needs.

Standardized education and training programs can ensure that health care workers possess the necessary skills and knowledge to provide high-quality care. Additionally, a unified system could offer better incentives and working conditions, reducing the brain drain of skilled professionals to other continents.

WHY A UNIFIED HEALTH CARE SYSTEM DOESN'T EXIST TODAY

There are many reasons we don't see a unified health care system across Africa today. Historically, colonial legacies have left many nations with fragmented and underdeveloped health infrastructures. Political instability and conflicts further strain resources and impede the development of comprehensive health policies. Economic constraints and competing priorities often result in health care receiving less attention and funding. And, as with any system, the diversity of languages, cultures, and governance styles makes standardization a complex endeavor.

MOVES TOWARD A UNIFIED HEALTH CARE SYSTEM

Despite these challenges, there are promising moves toward greater health care integration in Africa. The African Union's Agenda 2063 outlines a vision for a healthy and prosperous Africa, emphasizing the importance of health as a cornerstone for development. Initiatives like the African Continental Free Trade Area could potentially improve access to medicines and medical supplies by reducing trade barriers and fostering economic growth.

LOOKING OUTWARD FOR INNOVATION

While we may well look to more developed countries for a health care blueprint, they may not have all the answers. It is my belief that Africa needs to forge its own way based on its own unique diverse needs and resources and that looking to what others have done is not the best remedy.

Health care in the US is notoriously polarizing, with many on low incomes woefully unable to access affordable care. In the UK, the well-intended National Health Service provides health care free at the point of access to everyone, but it is under enormous strain, and patients wait many months, if not years, for treatment. It is deemed, by many, not to be fit for purpose.

The role of pharmaceutical giants in health care systems can affect the care that patients are able to access and at what cost, and trends in global government's policies affect health priorities for entire nations. Africa may learn from many non-African countries, but it should forge its own unique way, as, frankly, no one else has it down perfectly.

REMOVING BLOCKERS AND ACHIEVING A UNIFIED HEALTH SYSTEM

Investing in health infrastructure, workforce training, and technology is crucial to building resilient health systems, and, as with education and defense, public–private partnerships can play a vital role in ensuring health care services are both accessible and sustainable. Prioritizing health in national and regional development agendas can drive the necessary political will and financial commitment.

My key focus area, though, would be homegrown health technology investment. I would encourage inward investment in the region's already booming health technology sector and enable the plethora of exciting health start-ups to thrive.

THE ROLE OF THE PUBLIC SECTOR IN DELIVERING HEALTH CARE FOR AFRICA

The vision of a unified health care system in Africa is both ambitious and achievable. It requires a collective effort, driven by strong leadership, strategic investments, and innovative solutions. By building resilient health systems, Africa can pave the way for a healthier, more prosperous future. The journey toward this vision is complex, but the potential rewards are immense, promising a continent where every individual has the opportunity to thrive.

Innovation comes in the form of supporting start-ups and investing in the growing health technology start-up space. By doing so, Africa will build the health care systems that it requires, as opposed to importing models from elsewhere. Innovative start-ups will be able to respond to the exact needs of specific communities as well as more broadly. African ideas will solve African challenges.

I believe there are significant opportunities in the health technology space that go beyond even the great work I've described in the burgeoning health technology start-up ecosystem so far. I think to create a unified health care system that is fit for purpose, Africa needs to look beyond connectivity and mobile health (m-health), to look beyond simply moving brick-and-mortar concepts online by way of telehealth and online pharmacies, and create a new health blueprint.

RETHINKING VACCINES

The COVID-19 vaccine rollout exposed huge health inequalities between global nations, and sadly Africa lagged way behind the rest of the world. Africa's lag in accessing COVID-19 vaccines can be attributed to several factors, including economic disparities, logistics, supply chain issues, and geopolitical dynamics. The result was that many more people died who would have been saved had they had quicker access to vaccines.

The primary reason for the delay was, of course, money. Many African countries lacked the financial resources to compete with wealthier nations in securing vaccine supplies. High-income countries were able to purchase large quantities of vaccines in advance, often at higher prices, leaving fewer doses available for lower-income countries. Wealthier countries prioritized their own populations in vaccine nationalism.

Logistical challenges also played a role in distribution delays. Inadequate cold chain systems required for storing and transportation and lack of health infrastructure in remote areas further complicated distribution. Manufacturing bottlenecks, export restrictions from vaccine-producing countries, and the high demand from wealthier nations strained the supply chain, delaying vaccine deliveries to Africa. And, horrifically, vaccines manufactured in Africa were being shipped to the EU while Africans struggled to get vaccinated. I don't want to see that happening again.

To avoid the challenges experienced during the COVID-19 vaccine rollout, Africa must take a comprehensive approach that addresses the economic disparity, logistical challenges, and supply chain dependencies. A Pan-African unified health system can play a pivotal role.

Strengthening health care infrastructure in terms of upgrading facilities, improving cold chain storage, and enhancing transportation networks is vital. With a unified health system, these upgrades can be coordinated, ensuring uniform quality and efficiency across all member states. I would love to see Africa build and expand domestic pharmaceutical capabilities and reduce reliance on external suppliers. Securing adequate funding for health initiatives is essential. I would like to see African governments allocate a larger portion of their budgets to health care. A unified health system would facilitate collective bargaining with other nations.

African nations should collaborate on health policy. Regional bodies like the African Union and the African Centers for Disease Control and Prevention (Africa CDC) can facilitate collaboration and resource sharing. A Pan-African health system would go a step further.

RETHINKING INSURANCE

Health insurance is a major issue for Americans. It is expensive and divisive. For many, if you don't have a job, you simply don't have access to health care. And even if you do have a job, health care can cost you significantly. You need insurance just in case, but in my own experience of paying approximately $18,000 for a family of four, customers often feel shortchanged, especially if you are well. If you visit the doctor once a year, get a couple of vaccinations, a little physiotherapy, for example, but have no major diseases, $18,000 is indeed a lot to pay. It is simply out of reach for many people. Health care in America is expensive for many and abysmally unaffordable and therefore nonexistent for many others. Africa does not need a US-style system that would simply price most people out of healthcare. We must learn a cautionary tale from the US.

Is the US health insurance sector ripe for disruption? Well, innovations in health insurance are starting to reform the traditional health insurance model. Oscar Health[23] uses technology to simplify the insurance process, offering a user-friendly mobile app that helps members find doctors, manage prescriptions, and access telemedicine services. Clover Health[24] uses data analytics to improve care, focusing on preventative care and chronic disease management. The aim is to make health insurance more transparent, personalized, and efficient. Cheaper options are also emerging. For instance, high-deductible health plans (HDHPs) combined with health savings accounts (HSAs) offer lower premiums and tax advantages for saving medical expenses.

In Africa, innovative health insurance models are being explored to address the unique challenges of the continent. One such innovation is mobile-based health insurance. Companies like M-TIBA[25] in Kenya use mobile technology to provide affordable health insurance and savings solutions. M-TIBA allows users to save money for health care, receive health insurance, and pay for medical services using their mobile phones. It improves access to health care, particularly for low-income populations and those in remote areas.

Community-based health insurance schemes are also gaining traction in Africa. These pool resources from members of a

---

23 https://www.hioscar.com/
24 https://www.cloverhealth.com/en/
25 https://mtiba.com/

community to provide health care coverage, often with support from local governments. This model helps to make health care more affordable. In Rwanda, the Mutuelles de Santé[26] (Mutual Health) program is a successful example of community-based health insurance, providing coverage to over 80 percent of the population.

Another alternative model is "pay as you live" health insurance, which tailors premiums based on your lifestyle and health behaviors. This model incentivizes healthy living by offering lower premiums and rewards for maintaining good health. While still in its early stages, this approach has the potential to reduce health care costs and improve health outcomes. This model is seen globally and requires customers to use wearable devices in the form of fitness trackers or similar. For that reason, it comes with significant data concerns but is popular among many.

The pay as you live model is relatively new and is being explored and implemented in various parts of the world, including Africa. However, its adoption varies significantly across the continent. South Africa is at the forefront of adopting innovative health insurance models. Discovery Health's Vitality[27] program is a notable example. It integrates a wellness program that incentivizes healthy behaviors, rewarding healthy lifestyles with lower premiums and other benefits.

I believe to support health generally, insurers have a role to play in encouraging healthy lifestyles, but we must not do that at the expense of personal freedoms. There is considerable commercial value in collecting large datasets on population health; small reductions in costs are not enough of a value exchange for tracking intimate personal data long term.

THE ROLE OF TECHNOLOGY: INNOVATION IN THE HEALTH TECHNOLOGY SPACE

Technology is no longer solely the purview of Silicon Valley; indeed, the best innovation comes from solving real problems for

[26] https://en.wikipedia.org/wiki/Mutuelle_de_Santé
[27] https://www.discovery.co.za/business/vitality

real communities closer to home. And there is so much to choose from if you are looking to invest in the African health technology sector. It is booming.

Telemedicine is huge among start-ups founded in the last five years, with COVID accelerating this trend. Notable examples include Babyl[28] in Rwanda, Vezeeta[29] in Egypt, DRO Health[30] in Nigeria, and Zuri Health in Kenya. However, except for Rwanda, where Babyl has partnered with the government, most telemedicine start-ups are not yet integrated into national health care systems and rely on out-of-pocket payments from users.

Start-ups are also focusing on improving medical supply chains to ensure reliable access to drugs. Medsource,[31] mPharma,[32] and DrugStoc[33] are connecting pharmacies and clinics to suppliers, reducing price variability and ensuring product availability.

Start-ups like Rocket Health[34] in Uganda and Mydawa[35] in Kenya are enhancing access to medication through online pharmacies, helping combat counterfeit drugs. Indeed, there are estimated to be 160 online pharmacies[36] across Africa, showing the scale of the need and opportunity.

Digital tools for hospital, patient, and pharmacy management are being developed to streamline processes. Helium Health[37] has emerged as a leader, raising $30 million in Series B investment in 2023[38] from a range of investors.

---

[28] https://babyl.rw/
[29] https://www.vezeeta.com/en
[30] https://drohealth.com/
[31] https://www.medsource-group.com/
[32] https://mpharma.com/
[33] https://www.drugstoc.com/
[34] http://www.rockethealth.com
[35] https://mydawa.com/
[36] https://www.salientadvisory.com/reports/report-online-pharmacy-in-africa-regulatory-landscape-opportunities-for-action/
[37] https://heliumhealth.com/
[38] https://disruptafrica.com/2023/06/06/nigerias-helium-health-raises-30m-series-b-funding-to-expand-fintech-offering

I am encouraged by the fact that these start-ups and others are now part of a booming start-up ecosystem in Africa that is supported by significant private sector investment, demonstrating the commercial viability of new health care services.

Furthermore, initiatives like the HealthTech Hub Africa provide vital strategic support by way of start-up accelerator programs, nurturing early stage start-ups so that they can develop the products and partnerships to flourish and then linking them with government health initiatives:

> The HealthTech Hub Africa is a hybrid pan-African health tech accelerator, working to drive development of health technologies in Africa and fast-track these innovations in public health systems through collaboration with government partners and funders of global health. By doing so, the HealthTech Hub Africa aims to support African governments in tackling their largest health challenges, particularly those faced by low-income and underserved populations.

So, health technology start-ups get support to grow and connect with governments, and governments get access to the best innovation and ideas. HealthTech Hub's statistics are impressive: With 3.89 million direct beneficiaries, they've supported 3,800 health facilities and created 808 jobs.[39]

PUTTING DATA AT THE HEART OF HEALTH

As an advocate for putting data at the heart of any strategy, I want to explore the fact that data really does save lives. Data saves lives by transforming the health sector through improved patient care, more accurate diagnoses, and personalized treatment plans.

Harnessing data effectively can lead to better patient outcomes by enabling health care providers to make informed decisions

[39] https://thehealthtech.org/

based on comprehensive insights into a patient's health history, lifestyle, and genetic information. But to do any of that, you need to be able to collect, store, and analyze data in the first place, then act on it. I would like to see a data strategy as central to Africa's health policy and implementation. Data must be at the core of a new unified health system. Let's look at what's required.

Electronic health records (EHRs) are critical tool in harnessing data. EHRs compile a patient's entire medical history into a single, accessible digital record. This comprehensive view allows doctors to quickly access past treatments, medications, and diagnostic tests, which can prevent errors, reduce redundant testing, and ensure continuity of care. For instance, a doctor can use EHRs to track a diabetic patient's blood sugar levels over time and adjust treatment plans accordingly, leading to better management of the condition and preventing complications. Imagine if EHRs were in place across Africa; people would have streamlined access to the right treatment. It could save time and cost.

AI in the form of data analytics and machine learning is vital too; it's revolutionizing diagnostics and disease prediction. By analyzing vast amounts of health data, AI can identify patterns and correlations that would likely be missed by human observation alone. AI can process much more data than we humans. Algorithms can predict the likelihood of diseases such as cancer or heart disease by analyzing risk factors and early symptoms. This enables earlier intervention and more proactive management of health conditions, potentially saving lives by catching diseases in their early stages.

Data makes telehealth more effective: Wearable devices and mobile health apps can collect data on a patient's vital signs, activity levels, and other health metrics. Real-time data can be transmitted to health care providers, who can monitor patients' health remotely and intervene when necessary. For example, a heart monitor can alert a doctor if a patient's heart rate becomes irregular, prompting immediate medical advice or intervention.

Data also plays a crucial role in personalized medicine. By analyzing genetic information, doctors can tailor treatments to the individual's genetic makeup, improving the effectiveness of therapies.

Pharmacogenomics, which is the study of how genes affect a person's response to drugs, allows drugs to be personalized. This reduces the trial-and-error approach often associated with finding the right medication and minimizes adverse drug reactions.

Population health management can benefit significantly from data-driven approaches. By analyzing health data from large populations, public health officials can identify trends, track the spread of diseases, and develop targeted interventions. This approach was crucial during the COVID-19 pandemic, when data analysis helped track infection rates, identify hotspots, and allocate resources effectively. Vaccination campaigns and public health strategies can then be guided by data, leading to more efficient and effective responses.

Data saves lives by enabling health care providers to make more informed decisions, improving diagnostic accuracy, personalizing treatments, and enhancing public health management. The effective use of data can lead to better patient outcomes, reduced health care costs, and a more efficient health care system. As technology continues to advance, the potential for data to revolutionize health care and save lives will only grow.

EXPANDING TELEHEALTH

While there are many new ideas in telehealth, and telehealth is already successful in connecting many Africans to health care, there's more to be done. Mobile health initiatives are often organized bottom-up, rather than top down, mandated by governments. A 2021 study[40] showed that often it is personal mobile phones that are used by clinicians in a health care setting. And while mobile technology overwhelmingly positively impacted care, infrastructure was still a barrier to more effective use and adoption. For telehealth to be successful in a clinical setting, the infrastructure needs to be there. Doctors should not rely on their own mobile phones to do their jobs. So, while investment in telehealth services is welcomed, investment in infrastructure need to go hand in hand.

[40] https://www.ncbi.nlm.nih.gov/pmc/articles/PMC7903241/

DELIVERING DRONES

Another type of technological innovation already making an impact on African health is drones, which have the potential to revolutionize health care by addressing challenges such as difficult terrain, limited infrastructure, and logistical hurdles in delivering medical supplies. One of the most significant impacts of drones in African health care is their ability to deliver essential medical supplies to remote and underserved communities. Drones can quickly transport vaccines, blood samples, medications, and diagnostic kits to areas that are otherwise inaccessible or would take days to reach. During disease outbreaks, drones can deliver vaccines and medical supplies, ensuring timely immunization and treatment, which can prevent the spread of diseases.

Drones can also be used to transport samples from remote clinics to central laboratories for analysis. This capability is particularly important for diagnosing and managing diseases such as HIV, tuberculosis, and malaria. In this way, drones can expedite diagnosis and treatment, leading to better patient outcomes.

Drones also play an important role in emergency response situations. In cases of natural disasters, accidents, or medical emergencies, drones can quickly deliver life-saving supplies such as blood, plasma, and emergency medications to affected areas. This rapid response can be the difference between life and death in areas where traditional emergency services might be delayed due to poor infrastructure. Additionally, drones equipped with cameras and sensors can assess disaster-affected areas, providing valuable information for coordinating rescue and relief efforts.

Several African countries have already begun to harness the potential of drones in health care. For instance, in Rwanda and Ghana, drone delivery services operated by companies like Zipline have been successfully integrated into the national health care systems. These services have demonstrated the feasibility and benefits of using drones for medical deliveries, significantly improving the availability and accessibility of essential health care services in remote areas.

Despite the promising potential, there are challenges to the widespread adoption of drones in African health care. Regulatory frameworks need to be better developed to ensure safe drone operations. Investment in infrastructure, such as drone ports and maintenance facilities, is necessary to support large-scale deployment. Training for local personnel to operate and manage drone services is also important.

The potential for drones to transform African health care is immense. While they are not silver bullets and will not solve health care alone, they offer significant opportunities.[41] They offer a practical solution to overcoming logistical challenges, ensuring timely delivery of medical supplies, enhancing emergency responsiveness, and supporting public health initiatives.

IMAGINE HEALTH CARE IN 2050

People who live in a small village in Ghana in the year 2050 understand that health care is not a privilege accessible only to well-off middle classes, but something they can access with relative ease. Flexible, modern facilities equipped with the latest medical technologies, staffed by qualified nurses and doctors who can provide quality care, are all readily available—and not just in rural Ghana, but across the African continent.

Parents are able to bring children for routine checkups, confident that vaccines and treatments will keep their children healthy and thriving. People of all ages are able to access care, both during illness and into old age. A sense of security and well-being becomes the standard: Everyone has access to the care they need, when they need it. Care is universal and isn't determined by where you live or your income.

All Africans have fully funded health insurance. If you travel from Ghana to Egypt, your health insurance goes with you. You are able to access care, no questions asked. And if you live in

---

[41] https://blogs.lse.ac.uk/africaatlse/2024/03/06/drones-are-not-a-panacea-for-africas-healthcare-problems-but-offer-great-opportunities/

a remote area, you are also able to access care without having to travel long distances. Across the continent, a unified and connected health care system ensures no one is left behind.

THE REQUIRED MINDSET SHIFT

In order to create centralized and innovative health care for Africa, I'm advocating a range of measures that may require a shift in mindset. Health for Africa should not be modeled on health for Europe or the US. African health must respond to the needs and opportunities within Africa. The new united African mindset must reject the bad ideas from elsewhere and learn from the lessons of the past. Africa must not adopt a US style health insurance model; it needs a model that gives more people access to health care, not fewer. Africa must protect itself from the health inequality that came with the COVID-19 pandemic and ensure it can react to serve its own people. Agility is key to harnessing new technologies quickly and effectively: using telehealth to get healthcare to remote areas, using drones to deliver medicines and vaccines, using data to predict and prevent disease outbreaks—and all this needs investment.

From drones to data to telehealth, I would like to see the start-up ecosystem given more support, bringing in investment from global venture capital and private equity as well as financial support from governments. Health technology start-ups should be supported to develop public–private partnerships that could offer governments early access to innovation.

To achieve this vision, we need more founders equipped with the ambition and resources to be able to start new businesses. We need accelerators and incubators. We need investment. Start-up founders do not need mindset shift, but perhaps governments and policymakers do. If we accept that health equals wealth, shouldn't we be measuring health investment differently?

We should measure productivity and prosperity that comes from investing in health as well as measure direct health outcomes. We need a long-term holistic mindset if we are to realize this vision. Yes, it is about health, but it is also about so much more.

SECTION 4

SELF-SUFFICIENCY IN AFRICA

Chapter 11

LET'S UNLOCK AFRICA'S POTENTIAL FOR SELF-SUFFICIENCY

In a global economy, it may seem trite to discuss or advocate for self-sufficiency; of course, all economies operate within the global economy, so why seek to operate independently? While no country, continent, or trade bloc is totally self-reliant, there are varying degrees of autonomy. Those who enjoy the autonomy of self-reliance wield far greater power.

Imagine Africa becoming more self-sufficient—more self-sufficient in defense, in health, in monetary policy, and so on. Self-sufficiency is synonymous with control; if you are self-sufficient or self-reliant, you are empowered to make your own decisions to help you develop and progress. Self-sufficiency drives a more stable, prosperous future.

Africa's push for self-sufficiency is not just about reducing dependency but also about unlocking the continent's full potential. It is the key to ensuring that Africa can chart its own course and thrive in a rapidly changing global landscape.

WHY WE'RE HERE

Independence brought significant changes; however, the legacy of colonialism left many African nations with economies still structured to serve colonial powers, still focused on extracting raw materials and importing finished goods. The colonial economic model simply hindered development.

While independence allowed African countries to pursue their own development agendas, progress was hindered by political instability, corruption, and economic mismanagement. The lack of infrastructure and industrial bases, in many cases, made it difficult for African nations to achieve significant levels of self-sufficiency quickly.

In recent years, Africa has made significant inroads toward self-sufficiency. Many African nations are investing in infrastructure, renewable energy, and diversified local industries to reduce their dependency on imports. However, many African countries still depend heavily on foreign aid and imports. Several factors contribute to Africa's challenges in achieving self-sufficiency, including inadequate infrastructure, frequent changes in government, corruption, and short-term policies.

We all know what is key to become more self-sufficient, and that's to develop robust infrastructure, build a skilled workforce, reform policies, and cooperate (or unite) regionally as one nation. In striving to do those things, though, African nations are often tempted by so-called support from outside. Taking loans from the IMF is risky for Africa. But there are other risks too.

THE RISE OF NEOCOLONIALISM IN AFRICA TODAY

In rushing to secure support from outside, Africa risks not only reversing its self-sufficiency gains, but also risks welcoming in a new era of neocolonialism. Neocolonialism is using capitalism, globalization, cultural forces, and conditional aid to influence a developing country and is simply colonialism, but in a slightly new form. In neocolonialism, it is not only powerful nations that exert control over African economies, but multinational corporations too. Economic dependency through IMF loans, resource exploitation, political influence, cultural influence, and foreign-owned infrastructure are the hallmarks of neocolonialism in action today.

Colonial powers such as France and the United Kingdom continue to exert significant influence over African economies through established trade relationships, political ties, and financial dependencies. New powers like Russia and China are heavily investing in Africa, with China focusing on infrastructure, mining, and loans, while Russia seeks strategic military and resource-based engagements. The US also plays a crucial role, investing in various sectors and providing aid, but its involvement is often perceived as a balance against the growing influence of China and Russia. Alongside these traditional and emerging powers, countries like India, Japan, Turkey, South Korea, the UAE, and Brazil are increasingly investing in Africa, focusing on sustainable development, technology, and capacity building.

And it's not just countries. As I've outlined, corporations are heavily invested. TotalEnergies, for instance, has invested $6 billion to boost its oil and gas operations in Nigeria, including offshore oil projects and gas production assets in 2023.[42] Vodafone and its subsidiaries and Huawei have invested heavily in telecommunications infrastructure. Nestlé has been a long-standing investor in Africa, focusing on food and beverage production. China National Offshore Oil Corporation (CNOOC) is another major player, especially in oil and gas in countries like Uganda and Nigeria. And Anglo American and De Beers have substantial investments in mining operations throughout Africa. Overall, foreign direct investment (FDI) to African countries hit a record $83 billion in 2022.[43] And then there's Big Tech, with Alphabet (Google), Meta (Facebook), and others investing heavily.

THE ROLE OF THE IMF

What do you do when you want to invest in infrastructure and services and lift your country out of poverty but need financial assistance? You are likely to turn to the IMF for support. To be honest, I now consider this a necessary evil since educating myself about the IMF's mission and corrupt ways of working. This seemingly helpful organization, respected around the world, in many cases offers not assistance but hindrances to Africa. It is the source of support, but also great hardship and struggle. "The

[42] https://www.africanews.com/2023/12/19/totalenergies-ready-to-invest-6-billion-in-nigeria/

[43] https://unctad.org/topic/investment/world-investment-report

world cannot afford to continue throwing developing countries' plans and futures onto a raging bonfire of debt," said UN Secretary General Antonio Guterres in April 2024.[44] I want to look at why, now, over seventy years since its inception, the IMF is facing extreme criticism yet failing to offer a more sustainable way to support African development.

The IMF has played a significant role in African development since the 1960s. While plenty of people are familiar with the IMF and its role, plenty aren't, or at the very least their understanding is not high level. Sometimes it helps to go back to basics. All of us feel the effects of monetary policy and economics, yet these topics are opaque to most people. Many don't really appreciate the links among government policy, interest rates, currency valuations, and the price of goods and services they buy. And most people globally don't understand the intricacies of, or the interplay among, global organizations like the IMF and their own government and the impact that has on how much money they personally have to spend each week.

For the uninitiated, The IMF is an

> "organization of 190 countries working to promote international monetary cooperation, facilitate international trade, contribute to high levels of employment and real income, promote exchange stability, and help member countries address balance of payments imbalances. The IMF seeks to ensure the stability of the international monetary system: the system of exchange rates and international payments that enables countries and their citizens to transact with one another. All IMF member countries are represented on its Executive Board, which discusses the national, regional, and global consequences of each member's economic policies, approves IMF financing to help member countries, and oversees the IMF's capacity development efforts."[45]

---

[44] https://press.un.org/en/2024/sgsm22191.doc.htm

[45] https://press.un.org/en/2024/sgsm22191.doc.htm

The primary goals behind the creation of the IMF were these:

- Rebuild the international economic system post–World War II
- Prevent economic crises
- Provide financial assistance
- Promote global economic cooperation[46]

> *It aims to keep the global economy stable and prevent financial crises—an honorable goal, no doubt. How then, in 2024, were people rioting in the streets of Kenya about the appalling impact that the IMF has had on regular people there? How then, have people already in poverty been plunged into further debt with no clear path to clearing huge debt and no clear path to development and economic prosperity? Could this be why the IMF is seen as a force for evil?*

Let's look at just what this organization has done for Africa. The IMF's involvement in Africa was initially geared toward stabilizing the economies of African nations new to independence. In the years since it first got involved, though, the IMF's relationship with Africa has been marked by controversy. Criticism comes from everywhere, including from the UN, from academics, and from civil society.

And it's historical. In response to rising debt levels in the 70s and 80s, the IMF introduced the notorious structural adjustment programs (SAPs) across the continent. These programs aimed to restore macroeconomic stability through austerity measures and focused on reducing government spending. SAPs were criticized for their outcome on African people: Diminished public services led to increased poverty and social unrest. In the 90s, the IMF shifted its focus toward poverty reduction and sustainable development. Initiatives such as the Heavily Indebted Poor Countries (HIPC) were introduced to alleviate the debt burdens of the poorest countries, many of which were in Africa. In the 2000s, the IMF placed a stronger emphasis on economic reforms, capacity

[46] https://www.imf.org/external/pubs/ft/ar/2023/what-we-do/about-the-imf

building, and technical assistance, aiming to promote economic stability and reduce poverty.

Yet the IMF sees what it offers as helpful. Here's what they have to say about how IMF lending helps:

> IMF lending gives countries breathing room to adjust policies in an orderly manner, paving the way for a stable economy and sustainable growth. Policy adjustments will vary depending on the country's circumstances. For example, a country facing a sudden drop in the price of key exports may need financial assistance while moving to strengthen its economy and diversify its exports. A country facing severe capital outflows may need to restore investor confidence by addressing the problems that led to capital flight—perhaps interest rates are too low, the budget deficit and debt are growing too fast, or the banking system is inefficient or poorly regulated.
>
> Without timely IMF financing, a country's adjustment process may be more abrupt and difficult. For example, if investors are unwilling to provide new financing, the country may suffer a painful compression of government spending, imports, and economic activity. IMF financing facilitates a more gradual adjustment. Because IMF lending usually is accompanied by a set of corrective policy actions, it signals that appropriate policies are being put in place, encouraging the return of private investors. IMF lending also aims to protect the most vulnerable population via policy conditionality. In low-income countries, IMF lending is also typically meant to catalyze financial support from other donors and development partners.[47]

For those of us who aren't economists, I want to look at the mechanics at play here. What actually happens economically when a government takes a loan from the IMF? It's not just that

[47] https://www.imf.org/en/About/Factsheets/IMF-Lending

loans are often short term and need to be repaid before a country has had much chance to fiscally recover; the IMF is often criticized for devaluing a borrowing country's currency.

Indeed, IMF lending often includes conditions that require borrowing countries to devalue their currency, the rationale being to make the country's exports cheaper and more competitive on the global market. By devaluing a currency, the cost of goods produced in the borrowing country decreases relative to goods produced in countries with stronger currencies. The idea is to stimulate growth and improve trade.

When a country's currency is devalued, its goods and services become cheaper for foreign buyers. This can boost demand for exports, leading to increased production and potentially higher employment in export-related industries. For example, if a Ghanaian cedi devalues, Ghanaian cocoa becomes cheaper for buyers in Europe and the United States, potentially increasing sales and foreign exchange earnings.

A weaker currency, in turn, makes imports more expensive, which can reduce the volume of imports. This, combined with increased export revenues, can help improve the country's trade balance. For instance, if Ghana's currency devalues, imported cars, electronics, and other goods become more expensive, discouraging their purchase and encouraging consumption of locally produced alternatives.

However, devaluation has many significant downsides:

- Higher import costs: Essential goods such as food, fuel, and medicines, which many African countries import, become more expensive. For instance, if Nigeria devalues its currency, the cost of imported petroleum products rises, leading to higher prices at the pump and for goods that rely on transportation.
- Inflation: As import prices rise, the overall price level in the economy tends to increase, leading to inflation. This erodes the purchasing power of the population. A weaker currency can lead to higher costs for basic commodities such as maize (a staple food), and this affects food prices. Inflation affects the price of everything, for everyone.

- Cost of living: Higher prices for essential goods mean that people have to spend more to maintain the same standard of living. This is particularly harsh in economies in which wages do not keep pace with inflation. For example, devaluation might lead to higher costs for imported pharmaceuticals and increasing health care costs for individuals.
- Debt burden: If a country has borrowed in foreign currencies, a devaluation increases the local currency cost of servicing those debts. Imagine you borrow $100, but when you come to repay the $100 your currency is worth less than it was when you borrowed the money. As a result, you need to repay $150 or $200. A larger share of government revenue needs to be used to pay off debt rather than be invested in public services and infrastructure.

IMF conditions often impose devaluation intentionally. It is not an accidental outcome; rather, it is part of IMF strategy to encourage countries to right their economies in quick fashion. However, the immediate consequences of higher prices and inflation cause significant economic and social pain. As a result, these measures are controversial and challenging to implement without significant political and public resistance. In countries where many live in poverty, it simply cannot be acceptable that an international organization set up to improve global economic prosperity impoverishes so many millions with this approach.

While Africans (and others) have complained about this practice for many years, today the IMF's role in African development remains controversial. Critics argue that the IMF's policies still prioritize macroeconomic stability over social welfare. Plus, loan conditions can undermine national sovereignty and hinder governments' ability to implement their own development strategies. But why and how is this the case? How can an organization set up to stabilize struggling countries be doing harm? I think it's important to look at its structure.

The IMF is governed by its 190 member countries, each of which is represented on the IMF's Board of Governors and is run by an elected managing director, (currently Kristalina Georgieva from Bulgaria). However, not all countries have equal voting rights. Voting power is determined by a quota system. The larger the country's economy, the larger its quota. A few major economies therefore hold significant influence. The United States holds the largest quota, followed by Japan, China, Germany, and the United Kingdom. Along with France, Italy, and Canada, these countries hold substantial sway in decision making.

Due to their significant influence, the IMF often acts in the interests of its largest members. The US, China, and European countries are able to shape the IMF's policies and programs, prioritizing stability in global financial markets, aligning with their own economic interests. Policies imposed on borrowing countries reflect the priorities of major stakeholders, potentially at the expense of the borrowing nations' economic autonomy and development goals. As such, the IMF has been criticized as "colonial."

In response, the IMF is implementing new measures to support Africa. It is focusing on sustainable and inclusive growth. Initiatives include reforming concessional lending, reallocating special drawing rights to vulnerable countries, and creating the Resilience and Sustainability Trust to support long-term structural transformation.[48]

IMF Head Kristalina Georgieva said in 2022, "We at the IMF have taken unprecedented action to support our member countries, especially on the African continent. I like to say: we are stepping up with and for Africa."[49] Yet "the warning signs are all around us. In the past three years alone, the world has seen eighteen sovereign defaults in ten developing countries—the highest in two decades. And thirty-four of the poorest countries are either in or at high risk of debt distress."[50]

Indeed a 2023 report by Action Aid titled "Fifty Years of Failure—The International Monetary Fund, Debt and Austerity

[48] https://www.imf.org/en/News/Articles/2022/02/18/sp021822-stepping-up-with-and-for-africa

[49] https://www.imf.org/en/News/Articles/2022/02/18/sp021822-stepping-up-with-and-for-africa

[50] https://press.un.org/en/2024/sgsm22191.doc.htm

in Africa," published in 2024, shows that many African countries are moving fast toward debt distress. For example, Ghana was deemed sustainable in 2022 but was marked as being in debt distress by September 2023, with Kenya moving from sustainable to "high risk of distress."[51]

Action Aid explains:

> The IMF's standard policy advice and loan conditions that call for deficit targets at or below 3 percent of GDP are extremely conservative and reflect only one perspective in economics. African countries are in desperate need of scaled-up public investment in their health and education systems, national infrastructure, and human capital and there is no reason why their fiscal deficits should be constrained at such low levels. For the 40 years between the 1930s and the 1970s, more expansionary fiscal policy options (that allowed for higher fiscal deficits or for deficits to be paid down more slowly over time) were widely adopted around the world in high-income and middle- and low-income countries. Only with the rise of neoliberalism in the 1980s did such more expansionary fiscal policy options become side-lined, and the focus shifted to "deficit reduction" based on the monetarist idea that government budgets need to be balanced like household budgets—a view that has been widely discredited, but which still seems to drive IMF policy advice.[52]
>
> *Could the IMF's own strategy simply be outdated? Any positive change it may think it's implemented certainly isn't helping regular people in the African countries it has made loans to.*

[51] https://actionaid.org/sites/default/files/publications/Fifty Years of Failure - The IMF, Debt and Austerity in Africa_0.pdf
[52] https://press.un.org/en/2024/sgsm22191.doc.htm

I mentioned Kenya, a supposedly stable African nation; in the last two weeks as I write, Kenya has seen anti-austerity riots in which at least thirty-nine civilians were killed and hundreds were injured[53] while protesting a proposed 346 billion Kenyan shillings ($2.6 billion) tax increase imposed to repay the $2.34 billion loan issued in 2021 by the IMF.

In scrambling to pay back the loan, tax increases would hit the poor as prices of commodities would rise. President William Ruto withdrew the controversial finance bill following the riots.

According to Voice of America,

> Kenya owes $80 billion in domestic and foreign debt. Its debt stands at 68 percent of GDP, well above the World Bank and IMF's recommended maximum of 55 percent. The tax hikes were aimed at avoiding default and came after an agreement earlier this month between Kenya and the IMF on a comprehensive reform package. Most of Kenya's debt is owed to international bondholders, while its biggest bilateral creditor is China, to which it owes $5.7 billion.[54]
>
> *So it's not even that the IMF is Kenya's biggest creditor; Kenya is already borrowing from others. Kenyans are angry at the IMF for imposing conditions on its loan, yet there are other creditors to keep happy too. Such a system simply isn't decolonized; it's neo-colonized. What would it take to actually decolonize Kenya's economy?*

The neocolonial trap that positions Kenya as a source of cheap raw materials, and a consumer of northern industrial outputs, keeps Kenya at the bottom of the global value chain and exacerbates its debt crisis. Kenya's manufacturing relies

[53] https://depts.washington.edu/globalhealthjustice/kenyas-protests-the-violent-cost-of-imf-debt/

[54] https://www.voanews.com/a/deadly-kenya-protests-spurred-by-international-debt-woes/7677212.html

on imported machinery and fuel, further deepening trade deficits, weakening its currency, and leading to inflation and debt. Instead of following advice from local experts and Pan-African organizations, its leadership has followed advice from the IMF. To escape this vicious cycle, Kenya must invest in food sovereignty, renewable energy, and regional industrial policies for the long term. True economic liberation would require an alternative approach, including technology transfers, debt cancellation, and grants for renewable energy creation so that the country relies less on fossil fuels.

What if there was an alternative to the IMF? In terms of borrowing, it seems there already is (borrowing directly from foreign investors). And while I have focused on the actions and conditions imposed by the IMF, the conditions investors from China put on loans should be carefully scrutinized too.

Instead of an alternative to the IMF, perhaps a better question is "What can the IMF do differently in Africa?" and "What if the IMF canceled African debt?" My remedy for improving the IMF's impact would be for it to take a longer-term approach in Africa. By taking a longer-term approach in lending, there'd be less need for devaluation and less reliance on an already low-income population to shoulder the burden of rebalancing and repayment.

IMAGINING AN ALTERNATIVE IMF

Like most Africans, I would call for better terms from the IMF that reflect the needs of borrowing countries rather than the goals of Western lenders. There also needs to be greater transparency around loan conditions, both for borrowing governments and for the public at large.

Additionally, I would welcome strategies that made African nations more cautious about entering IMF-style agreements with other lenders, including but not limited to China. It's no good ending the colonial influence of one group to welcome it from another. Overall, though, the biggest single factor in Africa's development is currently debt. Debt holds Africa's development back and keeps it there. And of course, debt disproportionally affects women and girls. To combat this, I'd go as far as to call for debt cancellation.

If the IMF were to cancel African debt, it would significantly alleviate financial crises in many African countries; it would allow them to reallocate resources to critical areas like health care, education, and infrastructure development. It would substantially stimulate economic growth and stability, reduce poverty, and improve overall living standards. Fundamentally, it would allow developing countries to develop.

The IMF, though, is unlikely to cancel debt because it would set a precedent that could encourage fiscal irresponsibility and discourage future lending. Not all IMF lenders would accept losses though, and there are concerns about the impact on the global financial system.

However, several countries and organizations support debt cancellation for African nations, so there is a glimmer of hope. Prominent countries calling for debt cancellation are Norway and the United Kingdom.

And it's not just politicians calling for debt to be cancelled, the British public want debt to be canceled too:

> A poll of UK adults found that a high proportion (62%) of respondents considered it wrong that more than half of the countries of Africa (34) spent more money repaying external debt than on health, education, or combating the climate crisis. More than half of respondents (57%) considered it "absurd" that, in 2023, African countries spent 50 times more money on external debt than the entire UK aid budget for the year (£1.2 billion). Just under half (48%) believed that the UK Government should introduce legislation to ensure that private lenders play their part in cancelling debt; 45% that the UK should wipe the debts of lower income countries.[55]

[55] https://www.churchtimes.co.uk/articles/2024/24-may/news/world/british-public-backs-cancellation-of-african-debt

According to the International Development Committee of the UK Parliament, "The UK has already cancelled a large portion of its loans to low-income countries." It goes on to say, "The UK should work to establish a consensus with other creditors that such debt should be written off."[56]

UK politicians also support debt cancellation from other nations. The committee states, "A solution to the debt crisis cannot be found without engagement by and support from China. The UK government must engage with the Chinese government on debt relief for low-income countries both bilaterally and through the Paris Club.[57]"

The Paris Club is an informal group of creditors that work together to find sustainable solutions to payment difficulties experienced by debtor countries. Established in 1956, the Paris Club's main goal is to renegotiate debt terms to help countries restore economic stability. However, renegotiating and restructuring is very different form cancellation. I, along with a growing number of global citizens, believe debt cancellation is the path forward.

And therein is the key: What if it was not just up to the IMF to determine what was repaid and by when? What if the IMF had less sway in how African governments govern their countries and allocate resources? What if, instead of total IMF control, we leveraged public support from lender nations, like the 45 percent of those surveyed in the UK who believe debt to their own governments should be canceled? We need to listen to the people protesting on the streets of Nairobi, but we also need to listen to people in the UK and elsewhere where there is natural support for cancellation of debt and for the more effective development of Africa.

NEW INVESTORS, NEW RISKS

But what are the risks Africa faces when it relies too heavily on external support as opposed to prioritizing self-sufficiency? Here,

[56] https://publications.parliament.uk/pa/cm5803/cmselect/cmintdev/146/report.html

[57] https://publications.parliament.uk/pa/cm5803/cmselect/cmintdev/146/report.html

I explain the risks regardless of who the investor is. It could be China or Turkey, TotalEnergies or Nestlé, Google or Starlink.

A key risk is debt dependency: the potential to become overly indebted to new investors, especially when they invest the most, like China. Many infrastructure projects are funded through Chinese loans, which can lead to high levels of debt that may be difficult to repay.

With large amounts of debt come concerns about sovereignty. There have been instances when countries have had to cede control of key assets or resources to China when they failed to meet repayment obligations. For example, Sri Lanka had to lease its Hambantota port to a Chinese company for ninety-nine years due to its inability to repay Chinese loans, sparking fears that similar situations could occur in Africa. China seems to make the headlines when it comes to the risk of losing sovereignty, but others could also be in this position.

Heavy reliance on investment from one particular country can lead to economic dependency. If African economies become too reliant on funds from one nation, they may find themselves vulnerable to shifts in the economic policy or economic conditions within the lending country itself.

Additionally, foreign companies in Africa have sometimes been criticized for poor labor practices. Some have been accused of bringing in their own labor force rather than employing local workers, which can limit the economic benefits for the local population.

Political influence is another important risk. The economic clout of new investors from Russia, China, the UAE, and others can translate into significant political influence. Concerns that investments come with strings attached can compromise African political independence.

Of course, corruption is also a risk. While some deals from some investors come with anti-corruption measures, others don't. In terms of these deals, corruption would be on a grand scale, so it's vital there is transparency and that things are done properly to make sure investment goes where it was intended.

When it comes to technology, the exploitation of personal data can be seen as a form of digital colonialism, whereby African users become data sources without fair compensation or control over their information. The risk is that without proper controls in place, African users are simply exploited.

Furthermore, the algorithms and content policies of platforms like YouTube, Facebook, and X can influence which content gets visibility and which does not. This can lead to a situation when Western ideas are promoted and African content creators struggle to gain the same visibility and monetization opportunities as their Western counterparts. In this way Africans lose cultural influence.

Large firms in any industry can impede the growth of a homegrown industry. It is harder to innovate and enter the market when global players have that market sewn up. In this way there is also a risk of economic dominance and market control of foreign firms in African markets. Once these foreign firms have market dominance it becomes increasingly hard for new African firms to compete. By allowing large firms such dominance, we risk never being able to compete—and this goes for any sector.

And finally, there is a huge risk to African infrastructure. Any project that is owned by a foreign power, or a foreign company, may offer vital infrastructure, but it is the vital nature of it that makes it a significant risk. At any point, for any unknown reason, the investor may choose to withdraw access to critical infrastructure, wreaking widespread havoc. For example, by controlling the means of digital access, Big Tech companies can shape the online experiences and economic opportunities of African users. By controlling physical infrastructure, however, a company can also revoke access. Imagine what would happen if a company controlling the electricity supply of a nation decided that they wanted to turn it off. Even if they didn't take such action, being in such a powerful position also gives them significant political and economic leverage.

AS AWARENESS INCREASES, SO WILL RESISTANCE

Awareness of neocolonialism and its risks to Africa is growing increasingly among the general public. Demonstrations and debates indicate a growing recognition of neocolonial dynamics.

As there is increasing awareness, there can be increased resistance and more pressure put on leaders to reject the bad deals and equip themselves for increased self-sufficiency. This consciousness is vital for fostering a more autonomous and prosperous future for the continent and is part of the vital mind-set shift that Africa needs.

I strongly believe that Africa can navigate its way away from neocolonialism rather than falling into the new colonial trap set by investing companies and corporations. Africa can prosper if it has strong leaders who can negotiate better terms, based on a solid understanding of these risks.

Chapter 12

WHAT IF AFRICA'S INDUSTRIES WERE MORE DIVERSE?

When I consider the future for Africa's industries, robust and wholesale change is necessary. It's important to approach this issue with a growth mindset; just because Africa has a traditional set of industries it's been focused on for decades doesn't mean status quo is acceptable. Just because a country has a history in agriculture doesn't mean it can't radically develop its tourism industry. Just because another country is rich in minerals doesn't mean it can't become an expert in defense, or technology, or health, or manufacturing. Yet Africa is often perceived as being stuck with its traditional industries, so much so that change seems impossible and unlikely.

Historically, the colonial legacy, of course, shaped the structure of African economies, which were primarily developed to serve the interests of colonial powers, focusing on the extraction of raw materials and agricultural products for export. Post-independence, nations continued to rely on traditional sectors due, in part, to a lack of necessary infrastructure to develop anything else. A focus on the traditional, however, isn't currently serving Africa so well.

AFRICA NEEDS DIVERSIFICATION

Everyone knows Africa needs diversification, and here's why: The dependence on a limited number of commodities, such as oil, minerals, and agricultural products, makes African nations highly susceptible to global price fluctuations, which can lead to economic instability. Diversifying industries could stabilize income and reduce the threat and impact of economic shocks.

A diversified industrial base can also create a wide range of employment opportunities. This is particularly important given the current high levels of unemployment and underemployment across the continent. This would especially help the growing youth population to find jobs and meaningful careers.

In terms of Africa's rich supply of natural resources, simply exporting raw materials limits the value African countries gain from them. By developing industries that add value to raw materials through processing and manufacturing, African countries could retain more wealth and create higher-paying jobs than those necessary for export alone.

Diversification would also foster innovation and technological capabilities. Industries requiring various technologies and skills would lead to a more dynamic and competitive economy. Innovation is crucial for long-term economic growth and development. A more diverse economy can enhance regional trade and integration. African countries could produce goods to meet regional demand and reduce reliance on imports from outside. Ultimately, diversification is about reducing the risk of reliance on other economies, reducing the risk of economic shocks, developing potential for the future, and steadily increasing the wealth of all Africans.

WHY AFRICA HASN'T DIVERSIFIED ALREADY

For me, it's a total no brainer, so why hasn't Africa diversified? Even aside from the legacy of colonialism, the reasons for being tied to traditional industries are varied and complex.

Many African countries are heavily dependent on agriculture and mining for their GDP and export-related revenues. Agriculture employs a large proportion of the population, along with minerals and oil. The dependency creates a cycle whereby investment in these sectors is continually prioritized, often at the expense of other sectors such as manufacturing, technology, and services. In turn, fluctuating commodity prices can lead to economic instability, making it challenging to invest in and develop new industries, so the focus on the traditional industries means there's just no investment left to develop anything else.

Of course, Africa has rich resources and raw materials. It always has and always will, but we need to look beyond that if we are to successfully develop. My focus here, therefore, is on the other, newer complementary industries that will undoubtedly rely on and support the exploitation of Africa's natural resources rather than on resources themselves.

Infrastructure is indeed an issue. Without significant investment in infrastructure, transitioning to more advanced and diversified economic activities remains a challenge. And of course, education and skill gaps also contribute to the reliance on traditional industries. Until we develop structural opportunities such as my proposal of the skills farm idea to train people quickly and at scale, Africa will be unable to fill the skills gap required for modern industries.

But it's not just an economic issue. In many cases, some in positions of power benefit from maintaining the status quo. Corruption means some leaders discourage innovation and investment in other sectors—sectors they won't be able to directly benefit from. Corruption doesn't just stifle what Africa has today; it prevents Africa from grasping its future.

HOW AFRICA CAN DIVERSIFY ITS INDUSTRIES

Certainly, the groundwork needs to be put in place for diversification across the board. Any new industry requires a solid foundation, period. Robust infrastructure is critical for industrial diversification. Reliable transportation networks, energy supply, and communication systems are all key. Access to finance is essential for the growth of new industries. I would like to see better access to loans, grants, and venture capital for start-ups and small- and medium-sized enterprises. And that's for business development as well as research and development, which must be supported.

Africa must invest in education and training that aligns with the needs of emerging industries. Educational institutions and the private sector should collaborate to develop training programs, such as apprenticeships, to meet the requirements of new industries.

Reducing unnecessary bureaucratic barriers can also encourage entrepreneurship and investment. Ultimately, African countries need to improve the ease of doing business, and that includes putting in place anti-corruption measures to allow businesses to compete on a level playing field. The private sector plays a crucial role in industrial diversification. Political stability, though, is key to attracting inward investment from the private sector.

LESSONS FROM CHINA

Africa should focus first on infrastructure and then on manufacturing. Indeed, they each drive the other. And in developing its manufacturing sector, Africa can learn substantially from China.

China's manufacturing sector has undergone a remarkable transformation over the past several decades, transforming it into the world's leading industrial powerhouse. During the 1980s and 1990s, China established special economic zones like Shenzhen, which offered tax incentives and fewer regulations to attract foreign companies. This strategy attracted massive foreign investment and enabled massive industrialization and export-led growth.

In the 2000s, China became "the world's factory" we all know today, due to its vast labor force, improved infrastructure, and competitive pricing. In subsequent years, the sector continued to evolve with a focus on technology-related industries.

Today, China's manufacturing sector's ability to create goods at low cost makes it hard to compete with. But is there room for another manufacturing powerhouse, and could Africa follow in China's footsteps?

Well, the demand for manufacturing is increasing due to rising consumption, the need for supply chain diversification (global economies want supply chain protection in the event of unpredictable pandemics or conflicts), and technological advancements. Africa would be well positioned to meet this demand if it could expand its manufacturing sector. An expanded African manufacturing sector would drive economic growth, create jobs, and utilize natural resources effectively, strengthening the continent's role in international trade.

And the size of the prize is huge. As a powerhouse in the global economy, China produces about 35 percent[58] of the world's manufacturing output, making it the largest manufacturing nation globally. Over a third of everything manufactured anywhere is made in China. Indeed, manufacturing accounts for approximately 27 percent of its GDP, underscoring the sector's role in driving economic growth, employment, and industrial advancement.

In 2023 China's GDP was around $17.5 trillion,[59] vastly surpassing the combined GDP of Africa, which was about $3.1 trillion.[60] This is a huge disparity, underscoring the potential for manufacturing growth in Africa.

Africa could learn lessons from China, develop its skills and labor force, build infrastructure, and develop a manufacturing capability to rival China, at least in some verticals. What if Africa competed in some small way with China? What if it started making more electronics and household goods, not only for its domestic market but also for export?

Well, China needn't worry because the reality is China has its eye on another prize. ChapChina is not content with making

[58] https://geopoliticaleconomy.com/2024/01/31/china-world-manufacturing-superpower-production/
[59] https://www.china-briefing.com/news/chinas-gdp-in-2023/
[60] https://www.statista.com/statistics/1300858/total-gdp-value-in-africa

cheap stuff for the West, and with economic strategies such as the Made in China 2025 plan, China has its sights firmly set on upgrading its manufacturing capabilities and moving up the value chain.

The Made in China 2025 plan is a strategic initiative launched by the Chinese government in 2015 to upgrade its manufacturing sector and transform China into a global leader in high-tech industries. The plan aims to reduce China's dependency on foreign technology and promote innovation in various advanced sectors.

The key objectives of the Made in China 2025 plan include improving manufacturing efficiency, innovating in industries such as robotics, aerospace, clean energy, and biotechnology, moving to knowledge- and technology-intensive production, investing in research and development (R&D), and promoting environmentally friendly practices, all with the aim of reducing reliance on foreign technology and becoming more self-sustainable.

The plan has raised concerns internationally, particularly in the United States and Europe, due to its potential to create unfair competitive advantages for Chinese firms through government subsidies and protectionist policies. Critics suggest it might lead to market distortions and intellectual property issues. Despite its controversy, the plan underscores China's ambition to transform its manufacturing industry and move up the global value chain, shifting from being the world's factory for low-cost goods to a global center for high-tech innovation.

Africa can draw lessons from China's approach to infrastructure development, skill enhancement, and policy support to bolster its own manufacturing sector, but should Africa follow China's footsteps step-by-step, or should it leapfrog to a high-tech ambition from day one?

Developing manufacturing in Africa clearly faces challenges, such as the need for significant investment, skill development, political stability, and a conducive regulatory environment. With proper investment in infrastructure, education, and governance, Africa could overcome these barriers. While it may need to take baby steps at first, I advocate for a high-tech manufacturing strategy for Africa that could see the continent develop its capabilities quickly.

LESSONS FROM NATURE

We need new capability to drive growth in a range of emerging sectors, and we can, of course, learn from other nations, but we must not lose sight of lessons from Africa's natural landscape. While developing its manufacturing sector and moving "up the food chain" would be a formidable strategy for African development, we should also look downstream.

There could be a danger that African nations try to emulate nations in other parts of the world, with other opportunities and constraints. A diversification strategy for Africa must be Africa centric and Africa first. I want to look at how focusing on nature can be key to future innovation and can drive industry diversification in Africa. There are valuable lessons we can learn from our own geography and nature when creating our future.

The renewable energy industry is one case in point. Africa has not been at the forefront of fossil fuels and has not been proportionally responsible for climate change. Yet, it has significant power to fix issues for itself. Africa must look to its own natural resources as innovative solutions in the energy sector rather than follow in the footsteps of other nations.

To illustrate this point further, I'd like to introduce you to the concept of rewilding. In researching this book, I spoke to many political and business leaders, and one such business leader inspired me with a story about Kenyan tourism.

The tourism industry in Kenya is robust; in 2019, safaris accounted for 8 percent of the country's GDP. Eco-safaris protect the natural habitat, and, of course, all safaris ensure the wildlife habitat is preserved. But some go further. These landowners are not only in the business of conservation but also of taking farmed land back to nature. Rewilding is a conservation approach that involves restoring and protecting natural processes and wilderness areas to create more self-sustaining ecosystems. It involves reintroducing native species and removing human influence to allow nature to take its course.

By attracting tourists, rewilding can generate significant income for local communities and in turn fund further conservation efforts and support local businesses. Rewilding projects can create jobs in conservation, wildlife management, and ecotourism services. Plus, there are other benefits: clean water, fertile soil, and pollination, not to mention those projects providing opportunities to the local communities.

INDUSTRIES WITH POTENTIAL

So which industries should Africa diversify into? Africa has immense potential to diversify its economy beyond traditional sectors such as agriculture and mining, but where should it look for fresh innovation? Here's where I would start – see table 4.

Table 4. Sites for Fresh Innovation in Africa

Infrastructure	Infrastructure, infrastructure, infrastructure. It's key of course, and really needs to come first as it is an enabler of everything else. Improving logistics and transport infrastructure is essential for trade and other diversified industries, including manufacturing, agribusiness, renewables, and health. Indeed, it's crucial for economic growth.
Agribusiness and Agro Processing	While agriculture remains a significant part of African economies, moving up the value chain through agribusiness (the production, processing, and distribution of agricultural products) and agro processing (the transformation of raw agricultural products into consumable goods or other value) will be key. Developing this industry will enhance food security, increase export earnings, and create jobs.

Continued

Table 4. Continued

Renewable Energy	Africa has abundant renewable energy resources, including solar, wind, and hydroelectric power. By investing in renewable energy, governments can address electricity deficits, reduce dependence on fossil fuels, and combat climate change. It can also create the necessary jobs in construction, maintenance, and operations in this sector. African countries are already diversifying into this space: Kenya has invested heavily in geothermal energy, and South Africa has invested in solar and wind projects. Environmental sustainability is a key advantage of renewable energy. Africa is, after all, particularly vulnerable to the impacts of climate change, such as droughts, floods, and shifting weather patterns. By investing in clean energy, the continent can reduce greenhouse gas emissions and contribute to global efforts to combat climate change. What I would say about this, however, is that while Africa should harness its vast renewable energy sources, it must not be held responsible for fixing the climate change problem caused by others. Africa's renewable energy should be first and foremost for Africa.
Health Care	Investing in health care infrastructure and pharmaceutical manufacturing can improve public health outcomes, reduce the dependency on imported medicines, and effectively increase the responsiveness to health crises. A robust health care sector also contributes to a healthier, more productive workforce. Instead of Africa's talented doctors and health care workers leaving to treat patients in the US, UK, Canada, and Australia, I want them to stay because there's a growing health care sector at home.

Continued

Table 4. Continued

Tourism	Africa is a beautiful place and should be appealing to tourists from the continent and from afar. Yet tourism is nowhere near the levels enjoyed by Europe. In 2023, Africa had 66 million tourist visitors, compared to Europe's 709 million. Developing the tourism industry in Africa could drive economic growth and create employment opportunities. Tourists from traditional markets such as Europe, North America, and Asia continue to be important. This group is often drawn to Africa for its unique wildlife and safaris. But Africa should not look to visitors from oversees alone. The African middle class represents a growing and significant market for domestic tourism. With increasing disposable incomes, this demographic is eager to explore their own continent. The African diaspora is another vital market. These individuals have strong emotional and cultural ties to the continent and often travel "back" for heritage tourism, seeking to reconnect with their roots, visit family, and even invest in their countries of origin. Africa boasts some of the world's most exclusive and luxurious travel experiences, including high-end safari lodges and private beach resorts, so luxury tourism is a key sector. Medical tourism, educational tourism, and business tourism are other growing markets that Africa could easily develop.
Blue Economy	Africa's coastline stretches over 30,000 kilometers, with many countries relying heavily on their marine and coastal resources. The blue economy, therefore, is significant. The blue economy encompasses a wide range of activities, including fisheries, aquaculture, tourism, maritime transport, and marine biotechnology. The potential of the blue economy in Africa is vast. It could contribute significantly to food security and a reduction in poverty.

Continued

Table 4. Continued

Technology	Africa's technology industry holds significant potential for growth and development, and the approach to nurturing this sector should be tailored to the continent's unique challenges and opportunities. Africa's strategy should leverage its own strengths and address its specific needs rather than hope to emulate technology industries elsewhere. Countries like Nigeria, Kenya, and South Africa are already making strides in developing technology hubs in cities like Lagos, Nairobi, and Cape Town. These attract investment, talent, and partnerships. But while I often see technology hubs aiming to be the next Silicon Valley, I would hope Africa can find its own way with technology, creating technology for Africa rather than trying to emulate a model that is specific to a different set of economic conditions. Technology should not be seen merely as an industry in itself but also as a foundational element that can underpin and enhance other sectors. I have written about the investment required to bring connectivity to Africa and initiatives from global Big Tech companies like Meta and Google. I believe Africa needs to understand which technology it must develop itself and which it can rely on others for. Technology infrastructure enablers must allow Africa to develop its own technology rather than remain beholden to connectivity providers. So, technology absolutely must be developed, but as a way to support industrial diversification across the board, as well as an industry in itself. Africa needs a robust technology industry as "table stakes" to allow it to play in other areas.

Continued

Table 4. Continued

Manufacturing	Developing the manufacturing sector would reduce dependence on imported goods, considerably accelerate job creation, and drive industrialization. Africa's young and growing population provides a relatively cheap labor force that can be harnessed for manufacturing activities. The availability of so many workers could enable Africa to compete with other manufacturing-heavy economies such as China. As such, it would reduce reliance on goods manufactured abroad and enable greater resilience.

Chapter 13

WHAT IF AFRICANS TOOK BACK RELIGION FOR THEMSELVES?

I understand the profound role religion plays in the lives of many people, both in Africa and around the world. Religion can offer support and community; it can bring comfort and hope. However, I also believe that religion can be a double-edged sword, especially in Africa where it has often been used to control and exploit. While I am for religion if it brings good, I am vehemently against it when it causes harm. Sadly, religion can do a lot of harm, especially in Africa. When misused, religion (any religion) hampers Africa's ability to develop. It perpetuates divisions, it can be twisted to endorse harmful practices, and it can divert attention from pressing social issues.

While the core of religion may be well intended, its ability to be used to control populations and hold back development means it no longer serves people so well. In this chapter, I explore the radical idea of Africans reclaiming religion, reshaping it to serve their needs, foster unity, and promote development. By "taking back" religion, Africans can transform it into a force for good that aligns with their aspirations for progress and prosperity. First, I want to look at how we got to where we are.

A BRIEF HISTORY OF RELIGION IN AFRICA

Traditional African religions were and continue to be integral to the social, cultural, and spiritual lives of African people. They were practiced widely across the continent, with each region and ethnic group having its distinct traditions and practices.

Southwestern Nigeria and parts of Benin are home to the Yoruba religion, which is also known as Ifá. Often referred to as voodoo, Vodun is practiced by the Ewe and Fon peoples in Benin, Togo, and Ghana. The Akan people of Ghana and Ivory Coast worship the supreme god, Nyame. In South Africa, the Zulu people believe in a god called Unkulunkulu. In Mali, the Dogon people believe in Amma. In South Sudan, the Dinka people worship Nhialic. While all different, these diverse traditional African religions tend to share similarities, and many worship ancestors alongside gods and deities.

Before the spread of Christianity and Islam, there were many such religions throughout the African continent. They played a crucial role in shaping the cultures, societal structures, and worldviews of African communities.

Islam first surfaced in Africa in the seventh century, primarily through trade routes and conquests, but colonial interactions, particularly with North Africa and parts of West Africa, facilitated the further spread and entrenchment of Islam.

While Christianity had been present in Africa since the first century AD, it was the European colonial powers, especially the British, French, and Portuguese, that really expanded Christianity in Africa. Missionaries encouraged widespread conversion to various denominations of Christianity, including Catholicism, Protestantism, and Anglicanism.

RELIGION IN AFRICA TODAY

Today, Christianity and Islam are the most prominent religions in Africa, but indigenous religions are still practiced. Christianity is the largest religion in Africa, with approximately 631 million adherents, accounting for about 49 percent of the continent's population. Islam follows closely, with about 422 million adherents, representing 42 percent of the population. Traditional African religions are still practiced by around 8 percent of the population. A small percentage of Africans identify as nonreligious or adhere to other religions, according to the Pew Research Center.

Christianity is prevalent in Sub-Saharan Africa, in countries like Nigeria, Democratic Republic of Congo, Ethiopia, and South Africa. Nigeria, for instance, has a substantial Christian population, especially in the southern part of the country, and is home to some of the largest Christian congregations in the world. Islam is dominant in North Africa and parts of West Africa, including countries like Egypt, Algeria, Morocco, Sudan, and Senegal. Nigeria also has a large Muslim population, primarily in the northern regions. Countries like Somalia and Mauritania are almost entirely Muslim.

ATHEISM IN AFRICA

Atheism in Africa is relatively uncommon compared to other parts of the world. In the UK, for example, 37 percent of the population is atheist (made up of anti-theists, nonbelievers, and agnostics), whereas it's estimated that less than 1 percent of sub-Saharan Africa's population identified as unaffiliated with any religion.

Indeed, in many African countries, atheism can be socially stigmatized. Whereas religion provides a sense of community and identity, rejecting or questioning it can lead to social ostracism. In some countries, there are legal and political pressures that make it difficult to openly identify as an atheist. For instance, in some predominantly Muslim countries, apostasy, which is the act of abandoning one's religion, can be punishable by law.

RELIGION AS A FORM OF CONTROL

It's not that I don't want people to have religion, to take comfort and joy from it. If religion brings good, I am all for it. But religion has been used as a form of control throughout history, especially in Africa.

During the colonial era, European powers utilized religion to assert control over African societies. Missionaries were often at the forefront of colonial expansion, spreading Christianity alongside European cultural norms and values. Religious indoctrination helped to weaken traditional African belief systems and align local populations with colonial interests. Of course, the introduction of Christianity came with the suppression of indigenous religions. By converting Africans to Christianity, colonial powers could more easily manage and control the populace, as the new religion promoted obedience to authority and discouraged resistance.

After gaining independence, many African nations retained the religious structures established during colonial times. Political leaders used religion to legitimize their rule and maintain social order. For instance, in countries like Nigeria, where both Christianity and Islam are prominent, political leaders have leveraged religious affiliations to garner support and solidify their power base. Religious leaders, in turn, often wield significant influence over their congregations, guiding political opinions and behaviors that align with the interests of those in power.

Religion in Africa often dictates social norms and behaviors, reinforcing gender roles, family structures, and community dynamics. For example, in many Muslim-majority countries, Sharia law influences legal systems and societal expectations, particularly concerning women's rights and roles. Similarly, Christian denominations in Africa often promote patriarchal structures, whereby male authority is emphasized, and female subordination is encouraged. This all serves to maintain the traditional power dynamics and limit social mobility for certain groups, especially women.

Religious divisions have also been exploited to control and manipulate populations. In countries like Sudan and Nigeria, religious identities have been politicized, which has led to conflict and sectarian violence. Leaders use religious rhetoric to rally support and justify actions that consolidate their power while marginalizing or oppressing their opposition.

Religious institutions in Africa often wield considerable economic power. In many communities, churches and mosques are among the largest landowners and receive substantial financial contributions from their followers. Their influence is used to support political agendas, fund campaigns, and provide services that reinforce loyalty to religious and political leaders. By controlling economic resources, religious institutions exert significant influence over people.

In Uganda, the influence of evangelical Christian movements has been linked to legislative efforts to control social behaviors, particularly regarding LGBTQ+ rights. The Anti-Homosexuality Act of 2014, which proposed severe penalties for homosexual acts, was heavily supported by religious groups. This is clearly an example of legislation being used to control social behavior through religious doctrine.

THE PREACHER PARADOX

Whereas priests and members of the clergy in Europe tend to live very humbly, a troubling phenomenon has emerged in African Christianity, and that's the paradox of the wealthy preacher. How can African Christian preachers amass such significant personal wealth at the expense of their impoverished congregations?

The roots of the preacher paradox can be traced to the fusion of traditional African beliefs with Christian teachings. In many African cultures, spiritual leaders and healers have historically held positions of great influence and respect. This cultural backdrop has seamlessly blended with the rise of charismatic and Pentecostal Christianity, which emphasizes prosperity theology. Prosperity theory, if you're not yet a victim of it, is the belief that faith, positive speech, and donations to the church will increase one's material wealth. It's so successful as a theory and business strategy that you'll also see this in play in other realms, for example in the exploding self-help industry. Prosperity theory exploits those with less, but it resonates deeply with many Africans who face daily economic hardships and see their pastors as conduits to divine favor and financial breakthrough.

Preachers who exploit prosperity theology often promise miraculous financial blessings in return for generous donations. This creates a cycle whereby followers, desperate for change, give beyond their means, hoping for divine intervention. Churches exploiting the strategy frequently stress the importance of tithing, positioning these financial contributions as essential acts of faith. Followers give a regular percentage of their income, usually 10 percent, and contribute "seed offerings," a donation in expectation of a particular divine blessing. Consequently, many preachers amass significant wealth.

The growth of megachurches across Africa has further amplified this issue. Large congregations can attract tens of thousands of attendees, each contributing financially. The sheer scale of these operations allows for the collection of substantial sums of money. High-profile preachers, often with a flair for theatrics and motivational speaking, draw massive crowds and massive revenues.

The accumulation of wealth by preachers comes at a significant cost to their congregations. Many followers remain trapped in poverty, giving away money they cannot afford to lose. This financial strain can lead to neglect of essential needs such as food, health care, and education. The promise of future prosperity often keeps congregants hopeful but financially depleted.

The lavish lifestyles of some preachers stand in stark contrast to the living conditions of their followers. It is not uncommon to see pastors owning luxury cars, private jets, and opulent mansions. The ostentatious display of wealth is justified by preachers as a testament to God's blessings, which, in turn, reinforces the prosperity message.

To me, it simply raises ethical questions about the exploitation of vulnerable followers. I am absolutely horrified that these preachers can carry on unchallenged. In my mind, they are not helping their congregation but simply twisting religion to get rich while keeping their congregations poor.

The impact extends beyond individual congregations. It reflects a broader issue of income inequality and the misuse of religious authority. In many cases, these preachers wield significant influence over political and social matters, further entrenching their power and wealth. While most people don't even question their donations to these mostly men, something needs to be done to stop the practice. To me it simply screams exploitation.

I am in favor of encouraging smaller-scale, humbler churches and limiting the amount preachers can ask for as donations from their congregation. However, not everyone sees it that way and many have such strong faith in these preachers that they are happy to continue to give their money away in the hope it may bring them a better life.

CHURCH AND STATE

The religious composition and the extent to which religion influences governance in African countries varies widely across the continent. Some African governments are secular, while others are heavily influenced by religion. This religious influence impacts various aspects of life, including politics, education, social norms, and law.

Several African countries identify as secular states, meaning their governments officially separate religious institutions from state affairs. South Africa is constitutionally a secular state, ensuring freedom of religion and belief. The government does not endorse or give preferential treatment to any religion, allowing for a diverse society.

Although Nigeria is constitutionally a secular state, it has a complex relationship with religion. The country is divided between a predominantly Muslim north and a predominantly Christian south. While the federal government is secular, certain northern states have implemented Sharia law in addition to civil law. Kenya is also officially secular, with its constitution guaranteeing freedom of religion. Despite this, religious groups, particularly Christian organizations, exert significant influence on politics and society. Ethiopia's government is secular, but religion plays a significant role in the lives of its citizens. The Ethiopian Orthodox Church has a long history and considerable influence, though the state maintains a formal separation from religious institutions.

In some African countries, religion significantly influences governance. Until recently, Sudan was governed by Islamic law under President Omar al-Bashir's regime. The transitional government has taken steps towards secularism, but the influence of Islamic law remains strong in many aspects of life. Mauritania is an Islamic Republic where the government and legal system are heavily influenced by Islamic principles. Sharia law is applied alongside civil law, particularly in personal status matters like marriage, divorce, and inheritance. Somalia's provisional constitution recognizes Islam as the state religion and Islamic law as a foundation for the legal system. The influence of Islamic principles is evident in governance and social norms.

The influence of religion on governance in Africa impacts various aspects of life, from legal systems to social practices. In secular states, the separation of religion and state generally allows for greater religious freedom and diversity, fostering a more inclusive society. However, religious organizations and leaders still wield considerable influence over public opinion and policy.

DAILY CHRISTIAN LIFE

To illustrate the point about just how important religion is to the lives of Africans, I want to underscore how different being a Christian is in Africa from being a Christian in, for example, the US. In the US, you may go to church once a week, or you may not, but going to church is a distinct activity, and you would also fit in all sorts of other social activities in a normal week.

In Africa though, it's different. It's far more important and far more invasive. Christianity plays a significant role in the lives of many Africans, influencing their day-to-day activities. It is common for individuals to attend church at least once a week, with many participating in additional church activities, such as Bible studies, prayer meetings, and community service projects. Church attendance is not only a spiritual practice but also a crucial social activity. The church serves as a community center where individuals and families gather for worship, fellowship, and support.

The church plays a pivotal role in providing social services, such as education and health care. Churches run schools and clinics, offering essential services to the community, especially in areas where government resources are limited. Church, in Africa, is an integral part of daily life.

While I hope Africans get the support they need from their church, I fear that in addition to taking too much of their money to line preachers' pockets, they also give too much of their time and attention. If they spent more time on career development, on education, on supporting their own families even, they might be better able to develop their own prosperity and wealth. I fear the church asks too much of Africans, so much so that it is stifling personal and continental development.

RELIGION VERSUS LIBERALISM

Religious institutions hold substantial sway over political leaders and policies, particularly regarding social issues. One of the most notable impacts is the pervasive effort by religious groups to ban homosexuality across Africa. Religious groups often exert pressure on leaders to bring in laws that criminalize same-sex relationships, which they argue are necessary to preserve traditional values and moral standards.

Countries like Ghana, Uganda, Nigeria, and Kenya have seen intense lobbying from religious organizations outside the continent to pass anti-homosexuality laws. These laws not only criminalize same-sex relationships but also perpetuate discrimination and violence against LGBTQ+ people. This influence forces many to live in fear and secrecy; they are denied equal rights, employment opportunities, and access to services.

A more secular government, less influenced by religious dogma, would likely offer better protection for the LGBTQ+ community. Ensuring equal rights for all citizens, regardless of their sexual orientation, would be a significant step toward a more inclusive and just society.

Personally, I don't care who people choose to love or how they live their lives. I do know that inclusivity fosters a diverse and more innovative workforce, which is essential for economic growth and development in Africa. When people are free to express themselves and live without fear of discrimination, they are more likely to be productive, creative, and engaged in their work. Furthermore, protecting the rights of all citizens strengthens social cohesion. For these reasons, restricting religious influence on politics would allow Africa to reap the benefits of increased liberalism. This shift would not only improve the lives of LGBTQ+ individuals but also enhance the overall well-being and economic potential of the continent.

RELIGION HOLDS AFRICA BACK

While millions, perhaps billions would disagree with me, I want to explore the idea of religion as a negative force for Africa. Here, I've summarized the ways I believe religion holds Africa back.

Politicians often exploit religious sentiments to gain support, which can lead to sectarian divisions and conflict. Religious leaders use the support of their congregations to their advantage, blurring the boundaries between church and state and creating a political environment where decisions are made based on religious affiliations rather than merit or common good. In turn, this results in poor governance and corruption.

People taken in by religious dogma are often unaware of the extent to which they are being controlled and can easily be manipulated to believe in external threats or bad actors rather than understand the true situation they are in and who's responsible for it.

Religion can divert financial resources away from productive economic activities. While religious institutions do provide social services, the economic burden on individuals to support these institutions can be significant and keeps people in poverty, while religious leaders get rich.

Religion is so entrenched in many African cultures that it pervades every aspect of life and requires significant time to be dedicated to it. In turn this stops the African workforce from increasing its productivity. It's bad for business.

Some religion in Africa perpetuates patriarchal structures and gender inequalities. Some interpretations of Christianity and Islam promote traditional gender roles that restrict women's participation in the workforce. This can lead to discriminatory practices against women, limiting their access to education, health care, and economic opportunities.

Religious dogmas discourage critical thinking and scientific inquiry and promote a literal interpretation of religious texts that often contradicts scientific fact. This can limit educational advancements and hinder the adoption of modern technologies and scientific practices essential for development.

Some religious beliefs and practices can negatively impact health. For example, certain religious groups oppose modern medical treatments and vaccines, preferring faith-based healing methods.

Religion can be a barrier to social progress by maintaining conservative values that resist change. Issues such as LGBTQ+ rights, reproductive rights, and other progressive social policies often face strong opposition from religious groups, delaying social reforms.

The rise of religious extremism in some parts of Africa, such as the activities of Boko Haram in Nigeria, poses significant security threats. Extremist groups not only perpetrate violence but also disrupt education, health care, and economic activities, leading to instability and underdevelopment. Religious differences have been a source of conflict and violence in many African countries. Put simply, religion causes war and suffering.

BREAKING FREE AND TAKING RELIGION BACK

I am all for religion when it brings unity, hope, comfort, and prosperity. Sadly, though, I see religion bringing conflict, desperation, despair, and poverty. And I see it holding people from progressing. I want to advocate for secular governance that respects people's right to believe anything and allows religion to flourish as a force for good. I am not anti-religion. I am anti how religion is used and abused to control and indebt people.

Belief is very strong for so many, so I would have no hope of ever turning people away from religion; nor would I have a desire to. I would, however, like to see the day when religion is viewed in Africa as more of a philosophy—when people live by the positive values of their chosen religion and when they are protected from being exploited. This sadly needs some state intervention. I want to see the state intervening when congregations are robbed of their wealth to line the pockets of a few self-appointed leaders. I want to see the state intervening when there is the first sign of tension and conflict based on religious difference. I want to see the state intervening when religion impedes productivity, education, and growth.

I want to see people genuinely benefitting from religion rather than being brainwashed into thinking they are benefitting when in reality they are being held back. To get to a place where religion is a force for good, there need to be many changes. Africa can indeed break free from the negatives of religion, but it will need to do a lot of work. The following are some strategies that can help Africans break free from religion as a form of control.

It all starts with education; therefore, schools should be secular. I'd like to see education systems across Africa emphasize scientific inquiry, critical thinking, and secular values that can help counteract the limitations imposed by religious dogma. Curricula should include comprehensive sex education, scientific advancements, and critical thinking exercises to develop a well-rounded, informed population.

Laws that promote gender equality are crucial. Governments should work to eliminate gender-based discrimination and ensure equal opportunities for men and women in all sectors, including education, employment, and politics.

I'd establish strong, transparent, and accountable governance systems that can reduce the political manipulation of religion. Ensuring political decisions are made based on merit and the common good, rather than religious affiliations, can help create a more inclusive and equitable society.

We need to work together to tackle the root causes of religious extremism, such as poverty and unemployment, and reduce the appeal of extremist groups. Governments and organizations should invest in job creation, vocational training, and economic development programs to provide viable alternatives to vulnerable populations.

It's vital to encourage dialogue and cooperation between different religious groups from the ground up to help reduce sectarian tensions and promote mutual understanding. I'd develop and enforce laws that protect individual rights and freedoms, including freedom of religion and belief. I'd promote secular governance as a force for good, one that protects people's right to believe whatever they like, while ensuring governance is fair and transparent.

By adopting these strategies, Africa can address the negative impacts of religion while respecting religious freedom and promoting a more progressive, inclusive, and prosperous society. This balanced approach can help unlock the continent's full potential and ensure a better future for all its citizens.

Chapter 14

AFRICA'S YOUTH: NURTURING A UNITED MINDSET

Colonialism left many African nations with a fractured sense of identity, with division overshadowed by national and continental unity; this created what I call a divided mindset. However, Africa's youth have the potential to overcome these divisions and forge a new path forward, to develop and perpetuate a new mindset, and by doing so forge a new future—a united one. Indeed, Africa's youth will deliver the next generation of African leaders, and this generation of leaders will unite Africa.

Until they take up their future leadership positions, empowered young people can drive the movement toward self-sufficiency and economic independence. They can challenge the status quo, demanding more accountability from existing leaders and advocating for policies that prioritize African interests. As more young people take on leadership roles, they can help shift the focus from short-term gains to long-term sustainable development that benefits all Africans.

Furthermore, a united mindset among Africa's youth can help address the continent's political divisions. By fostering a sense of Pan-African solidarity, young people can work together to overcome the artificial borders and divisions that have hindered Africa's progress for decades. They can advocate for policies that promote regional integration, economic cooperation, and collective security, paving the way for a more united and prosperous Africa.

WE NEED TO FOCUS ON TODAY'S YOUTH

I criticized Agenda 2063 for looking too far out, for focusing too far in the future. Those who are in their twenties today will be in their sixties when the aspirations of Agenda 2063 come to fruition, if indeed they do. To me, it seems like we are signing up to fail a generation—or two generations. If you are in your forties today, as I am, Agenda 2063 suggests you will live in a united prosperous Africa only when you are in old age, if indeed you see it at all. Anyone over thirty, in fact, can really only benefit through their children and their grandchildren. If you are a teenager of fifteen today considering your future, you may even be approaching retirement by 2063; the promises will not have enhanced your skills, health, opportunities, career, or prosperity. If we believe Agenda 2063 will deliver, we can envisage a better Africa, but not for ourselves. We have to forgo that experience.

And while it is undoubtedly a positive to imagine a better Africa for future generations, shouldn't we all benefit in some way too? And shouldn't we all benefit soon? Shouldn't the young people in Africa today benefit? Indeed, a better Africa of tomorrow will require the young people of today to bring it into reality. We absolutely need young people to be on board.

Africa is currently experiencing a demographic shift of immense proportions, with its youth population growing at an unprecedented rate: around 2.5 percent per year, significantly higher than the global average. By 2050, the continent's population is projected to double, with a significant majority under the age of twenty-five. By 2063, Africa's population is on target to reach 3 billion people,[61] although the exact figure will depend on various factors such as birth rates, mortality rates, and migration patterns.

OPPORTUNITIES FOR YOUNG PEOPLE TODAY

Of course, Africa's youth hold the key to the continent's future prosperity. With the right investments in education, skills

[61] https://futures.issafrica.org/thematic/03-demographic-dividend/

development, and entrepreneurship, young people will drive economic growth, technological innovation, and social transformation. The potential is immense; African youth are already tech savvy, entrepreneurial, and connected to global trends. Many are creating innovative solutions to local problems; many are already operating in the global marketplace through online platforms. They can see a global opportunity, they can see the skills they need to develop, and some of them, those who are able to access robust enough connectivity and who have been lucky enough to access the right education and skills, they are operating in the global digital workforce already.

The real opportunity though, is that Africa's youth population presents a vast and dynamic labor force within Africa, in brick-and-mortar businesses, not just online. With proper vocational training and education, Africa's young people could fill skill gaps in key sectors such as agriculture, manufacturing, and technology and drive industrialization and diversification.

This could reduce the continent's reliance on raw material exports and help build resilient, diversified economies while keeping young talent in Africa instead of seeing educated young people leave to seek their fortunes elsewhere. Young people really are the key, and we need to help them shift from unskilled to skilled jobs now—today.

CHALLENGES FACING YOUNG PEOPLE

Sadly, today many are still left behind, unable to access the education they need to thrive, to be economically active, to contribute to creating a prosperous continent. Access to quality education is particularly difficult to come by in rural areas. High unemployment rates are a critical issue, and many young Africans in rural areas and elsewhere simply won't be able to find work because there just isn't enough of it to go around. Governments are struggling to create enough jobs to make full use of the growing potential workforce. Of course, if you haven't been able to access education to equip you with relevant and valuable skills, and if you can't find a job, skilled or otherwise, you might well feel disenfranchised. You may seek work elsewhere, or you might simply fall out of the workforce. For young people to leave the workforce, to not be offered the opportunities their counterparts elsewhere in the world are offered is a travesty, but an all too familiar one.

Once someone has been failed by the education system, they become harder to reach. If they are not thriving in a meaningful career, if they are disenfranchised, any desire to become involved in politics, or desire to contribute to the prosperity of future generations, will understandably wane. Failing to support young people harms them. Yet it may strengthen the existing power structures and allow poor leaders to lead poorly for longer. Perversely, failing to support young people to fully engage in their communities and economies could even be a strategy by some unscrupulous leaders for amassing more personal wealth by clinging onto power.

So, are young people encouraged not to participate in the political process? Are they intentionally turned off to politics? Well, it's true young people tend not to be very involved in the political process across the continent, even while they make up the majority of the population. Traditional structures of power do indeed see older generations dominating leadership roles; youth voices are marginalized.

Young people in Africa today are able to see the opportunities afforded to young people elsewhere in the world. They are tantalized by platforms offering them a fair deal in a global economy, but they don't all have the skills or the infrastructure to make full use of it. They are all aware of local politics and are all able to leverage social media to learn more and to mobilize, but they are also heavily penalized for challenging the status quo.

Put simply, young people are un-empowered. Many are disenfranchised. At the very least they are all dissatisfied with how things are, not least because they fully understand how much better their opportunities, wealth, health, and continent, could be. Yet while they can see what others have elsewhere, while they can see how they could contribute to a better Africa, they are not participating, at least not on the scale needed to create a radical shift.

GREEN SHOOTS AND GRASS ROOTS

I don't want to paint a picture too bleak. While I think political engagement is low, there are green shoots of change, there is social engagement and social activism, and there is hope. Social media has given young Africans a platform to voice their concerns, mobilize around causes, and hold leaders accountable. Youth activism in Africa has seen many successful examples across the continent, as young people have played pivotal roles in advocating for change, social justice, and political reform. There are many notable examples.

Organizations like Youth Congress[62] and Siasa Place[63] are empowering young people to participate in politics and understand their rights and responsibilities as citizens in Kenya. Youth Congress increased the number of youths running for elective seats from 3,438 in 2017 to 4,350 in 2022. The Uraia Trust[64] delivers a civic engagement program and works with young people to enhance their understanding of human rights, governance, and democracy. Such programs empower the youth to hold leaders accountable and to participate meaningfully in the democratic process.

The "Fees Must Fall"[65] student-led protest movement in South Africa launched in 2015 and advocated against the increase in university fees and the broader issue of affordable higher education. The movement successfully pressured the South African government to freeze tuition fee increases and sparked a national dialogue on the costs and accessibility of education while also highlighting issues of institutional racism and the legacy of apartheid in education.

62 https://theyouthcongress.org/

63 https://siasaplace.com/

64 https://uraia.or.ke/

65 https://www.globalcitizen.org/en/content/south-africa-student-protests-explained/

In 2011 Y'en a Marre,[66] meaning "We're Fed Up," mobilized young people in Senegal to demand better governance, transparency, and an end to corruption. It played a crucial role in opposing President Abdoulaye Wade's attempt to seek a third term in 2012 and ultimately contributed to his defeat at the ballot box.

Balai Citoyen[67] in Burkina Faso was cofounded in 2013 by musicians Smockey and Sams'K Le Jah and emerged as a powerful force against the long-standing presidency of Blaise Compaoré, who had been in power for twenty-seven years. It played a significant role in the 2014 uprising that led to his resignation, a historic moment for democracy in Burkina Faso.

#BringBackOurGirls[68] in Nigeria was set up in 2014 following the Boko Haram kidnapping. Led by Nigerian activists such as Oby Ezekwesili,[69] it drew international attention to the plight of the kidnapped girls and highlighted issues of terrorism, gender violence, and education in Nigeria. The campaigns undoubtedly contributed to the eventual release of some of the abducted girls.

The #EndSARS[70] protests were led by Nigerian youth in 2020 and were successful in drawing global attention to governance in Nigeria and achieving the disbandment of the Special Anti-Robbery Squad (SARS), a police unit accused of brutality, extortion, and extrajudicial killings.

The issue of climate change, too, has seen African youth get fully involved. Vanessa Nakate,[71] a Ugandan climate justice activist, has brought attention to the disproportionate impact of climate change on African countries. Elizabeth Wathuti[72] from Kenya founded the Green Generation Initiative, raising awareness about environmental issues and advocating for sustainable practices.

---

66 https://en.wikipedia.org/wiki/Y'en_a_Marre
67 https://lebalaicitoyen.fr/
68 https://bringbackourgirls.ng/
69 https://en.wikipedia.org/wiki/Oby_Ezekwesili
70 https://en.wikipedia.org/wiki/End_SARS
71 https://en.wikipedia.org/wiki/Vanessa_Nakate
72 https://en.wikipedia.org/wiki/Elizabeth_Wathuti

Youth activism is successful in challenging the status quo, advocating for social justice, and driving political change. Through grassroots organization and social media, African youth have shown their ability to influence national and international agendas. Their activism often leads to significant reforms and societal shifts.

THE DANGERS IN DISRUPTION

Meaningful political engagement is sadly fraught with challenges. It is dangerous. Young activists often face repression, with governments using censorship, surveillance, and even violence to suppress dissent. We need to make activism safe. We need to expect, no, invite, discussion, debate, activism, and protest. We need to hear it. We need to listen, and we need to act.

Young people in Africa face far greater challenges than their counterparts in, for example, the US or Europe when it comes to effective and safe activism. Most young people in Western countries expect they can attend rallies and peacefully protest without the fear of government reprisals. Yet young people in Africa don't always have the same liberties. Involvement in activism in Africa comes with considerable risks.

In Zimbabwe, young activists have faced state repression and violence; during protests against President Robert Mugabe in 2016, many activists were arrested and tortured, and some even disappeared. In Nigeria, the #EndSARS protests opposing police brutality in 2020 ended in tragedy when security forces opened fire on unarmed protesters at the Lekki Toll Gate in Lagos. Twelve protesters were killed.

Legal risks also pose significant challenges for young activists. In Uganda, Bobi Wine,[73] a musician turned politician, became a symbol of youth resistance against President Yoweri Museveni's regime. His activism led to house arrest, charges, and brutal treatment by authorities. In Egypt, during the Arab Spring in 2011, many young activists faced long prison sentences under charges

---

[73] https://bobiwine.com/

like "spreading false news" or "inciting protests." Indeed, during the course of writing this book, Bobi Wine was shot; he claims someone "made an attempt on his life."[74]

In addition to physical and legal threats, activists in Africa can also face an economic backlash. In Sudan, during the protests that led to the ousting of President Omar al-Bashir in 2019, of the young protesters who were not killed by police, many lost their jobs or were expelled from universities due to their involvement in the movement. In Kenya, youth activists have faced cyberattacks, hacking, and surveillance, particularly during election periods.

In more extreme cases, the risks escalate to targeted attacks and loss of life. In Cameroon, youth activists advocating for the rights of the English-speaking population were kidnapped, tortured, and killed in 2018.[75]

African youth involved in activism face severe risks. I find it tragic that young people can't participate in driving change safely and that many risk their lives to do so. We clearly need stronger protections and support systems for those advocating for social and political reforms. Instead of attempting to stifle change with violence, we should be inviting young people to engage and participate; we should be welcoming the change that is necessary. We should be uniting Africa's youth to create a stronger Africa for all.

A PATH TO A UNITED MINDSET

Young people are undoubtedly the key to the success of the continent in 2063, in 2050, and indeed now. We must respect them, engage them, and allow them to help shape the future, for themselves and for future generations. We must not leave them behind. We need to break down the barriers that prevent them from participating fully in the political process by not only

---

[74] https://www.theguardian.com/world/article/2024/sep/03/ugandan-opposition-leader-bobi-wine-shot-in-leg-after-police-confrontation

[75] https://www.voanews.com/a/dozens-of-cameroon-youth-killed-in-south/4411815.html

creating more opportunities for young people to get involved in leadership but also by addressing the structural inequalities that limit their access to education, employment, and political power.

The Arab Spring saw uprising and the overthrow of governments in the Arab world, yet plenty of the overthrown leaders were Africans. Zine al-Abidine Ben Ali of Tunisia was the first leader to be ousted after a twenty-three-year rule. Hosni Mubarak was deposed in Egypt following eighteen days of mass protests and nearly thirty years in power. Muammar Gaddafi's Libyan regime was overthrown after months of armed conflict ending his forty-two-year rule.

In 2024, with increasing protests in Africa, commentators wonder whether we are heading for an African Spring.[76] I want to see change, but I want to see change in a controlled, safe way. I want all stakeholders to be involved and supported. I don't want to see violence, brutality, or loss of life. My route to change is through involving and engaging young people, helping them to participate, helping them to shift the mindset from divided to united.

The path will not be fully clear, yet we must have the vision to move forward. The path will not be easy, yet we must start with practical changes. The path will be littered with obstacles, yet we must be prepared to navigate toward our goal. The path will instill fear, yet we must find our courage.

While I cannot provide a long-term plan for how to achieve a united mindset, I can provide a plan for engaging Africa's youth. I don't want to create something so complex that it needs global stakeholders to give the go ahead. I don't want to create something so enormous that it'll take decades to see fruition. Instead, I have a simple, clear plan for engaging the young people of Africa. I call it the "United Manifesto."

---

[76] https://www.aljazeera.com/features/2024/8/12/is-africa-experiencing-a-protest-led-revolution

Chapter 15

A UNITED MANIFESTO

My United Manifesto is a five-point plan for engaging young people in politics and, in turn, uniting a continent in years not decades. I want to see a united Africa. I want to see young people afforded unbounded opportunity. I want to see all Africans prosper.

To achieve any of this, we need to shift the African mindset from divided to united. To achieve that, we need to start afresh, to start with Africa's youth. Young people must be engaged in politics, in forging a new political system, in creating and sustaining great change.

This is a call to the young people of Africa. If you are old enough to be interested in your future, in politics, in the safety of your family, in your ability to develop your skills, to forge a career, to create wealth and prosperity, to contribute to a better Africa for all, then call for these five things. This is for you.

This is also a call to all African leaders, to all those involved in politics at any level, a call to community leaders who can encourage young people to get involved. If you want to create a prosperous Africa. If you want to do this without hardship or bloodshed, this is for you. To shift the African mindset from divided to united, we must

- increase engagement with citizens, especially the African youth;
- improve the transparency of our finances and politics;
- track our progress towards a united Africa;
- accelerate skills for all; and
- harness youth leadership for now and the future.

INCREASING ENGAGEMENT

We must increase engagement with citizens, especially the African youth. Increasing engagement is the most vital step in shifting the African mindset from divided to united.

We need to see these things:

- Awareness of political issues
- Understanding of the potential of social activism
- Ensured safety for young people involved in social activism and peaceful protest

We can achieve this through the following:

- Awareness campaigns
- Updates to school curricula
- An Africa United platform

Awareness Campaigns

Just as organizations like Uraia[77] and the Emerging Leaders Foundation Africa[78] are developing civic engagement, we need to see this on a Pan-African scale. Public awareness campaigns are required on key issues:

- Corruption: Helping young people to demand better standards from those in power
- Economics: Helping citizens to properly understand the economic impact of government borrowing, debt, inflation, devaluation, and cost-of-living increases
- Foreign investment: Helping everyone understand the opportunities and threats from foreign investment
- Diversification: Helping people understand the future opportunities they could access from diversified industries and setting out clear educational and skills paths.

---

[77] https://uraia.or.ke/

[78] https://elfafrica.org/governance-and-civic-engagement

Updates to School Curricula

Politics should be a compulsory subject in the school curriculum in all African countries, as it should be, but often isn't globally. Young people should be equipped with a comprehensive understanding of the political landscape and the opportunities for Africa's development.

An Africa United Platform

An African-owned social media platform that connects young people across the continent could be instrumental in engaging young people, supporting their involvement in politics, increasing the transparency and accountability of existing systems, and helping to educate the next generation. There is no current space young people can go to for independent, verified and verifiable, unbiased news and facts on the state of their economies, politics in their region, or the progress their leaders are making on their commitments. Furthermore, there is no safe space where citizens can go to access unbiased news. I would love to see a platform that was not influenced by the foreign state–owned bot farms that influence all our social media feeds today. I would love to see a platform that has the best interests of African citizens at heart, as opposed to one that can be used by bad actors to manipulate the hearts and minds of Africa's youth to their own ends.

An Africa United Platform would contain special interest groups to connect communities, fact checked data, a space for leaders to share transparent data and progress updates, and opportunities for young people to get involved in local, national, and continental politics in a safe way. Such a platform would also allow political leaders to tap into the zeitgeist, to better understand what matters most to citizens, especially young people. They would be able to undertake surveys and polls, test policies and messaging, and understand and serve their people better.

INCREASING TRANSPARENCY

We must improve the transparency of our finances and politics, of our deals and investments, and of our decision-making processes to ensure that every action taken by our leaders is done with the full knowledge and consent of the people. I believe that African citizens, especially young people, deserve to know how their political leaders spend money, just like citizens do in other countries in other parts of the world. Simply, Africans deserve transparency.

Transparency is the cornerstone of trust in governance and the bedrock of a functioning democracy. For Africa to prosper, there must be a concerted effort to increase transparency at all levels of government and within the private sector. We need to see these things:

- Full disclosure of government revenues, expenditures, and contracts
- Transparent public procurement processes
- Transparent and accessible financial reporting
- Open data

We can achieve this through the following:

- Implementing blockchain technology in financial systems and public procurement
- Mandating the publication of government financial data in open formats
- Establishing independent anti-corruption agencies
- Implementing blockchain technology in financial systems and public procurement

Blockchain technology offers a unique solution to many of the transparency challenges. By leveraging blockchain, governments can create immutable records of financial transactions and public procurement processes. This level of transparency would make it nearly impossible to alter or falsify records, thereby reducing opportunities for corruption.

MANDATING THE PUBLICATION OF GOVERNMENT FINANCIAL DATA

To build trust, governments must be more transparent about how public funds are collected and spent. They must regularly publish detailed reports on government revenues, expenditures, and debts, available in user-friendly formats accessible to all. Public contracts, including those with private companies, should be disclosed, as should politician and civil servant remuneration; after all, they work for you.

ESTABLISHING INDEPENDENT ANTI-CORRUPTION AGENCIES

Anti-corruption agencies should be strengthened, and where they do not exist should be set up. Agencies should be free from political influence, have the resources needed to carry out their work effectively, and be mandated to make their findings public.

TRACKING PROGRESS

We must track our progress towards a united Africa. Just as we need transparency in our finances and politics, it's crucial we track and communicate the progress of our initiatives, policies, and development goals. Without measurable outcomes, we risk stagnation and inefficiency, leaving our people without the promised improvements. Tracking progress is not just about meeting targets; it's about ensuring that the resources, time, and efforts invested by our governments yield real, measurable improvements in the lives of African citizens. By establishing these systems and holding ourselves accountable, we can build a continent that not only dreams of greatness but also achieves it. All Africans should be aware of our progress toward a better future.

We need to see these things:

- Development indicators and targets
- Progress reports
- Performance metrics for public services
- Outcomes of government initiatives

We can achieve this through the following:

- Establishment of a centralized data and analytics platform
- Regular public progress reports
- Independent audits and reviews

Centralized Data and Analytics Platform

A centralized data platform is essential for gathering, analyzing, and sharing key metrics. Such a platform could track everything from health outcomes and education levels to economic performance and infrastructure projects. By making data publicly accessible, citizens can see the tangible impacts of government policies and hold leaders to account.

Regular Public Progress Reports

Governments should commit to issuing regular progress reports that detail the status of key projects and initiatives. Reports must be clear, concise, and free from jargon, allowing every citizen to understand how their country is advancing.

Independent Audits and Reviews

To ensure that the progress being reported is accurate and unbiased, independent audits and reviews should be conducted regularly by third-party organizations with no ties to the government.

ACCELERATING SKILLS

We must accelerate skills for all. For Africa to fully realize its potential and take its rightful place on the global stage, we must focus on accelerating skills across the continent. The future belongs to those who are prepared, and in a world driven by technology, innovation, and knowledge, our people must be equipped with the skills that will allow them to thrive in a rapidly changing environment. We must implement strategies that not only educate but also empower Africans to be leaders, innovators, and entrepreneurs.

Accelerating skills development is not just about preparing our people for jobs; it's about equipping them with the tools they need to create jobs, to lead, and to drive the continent forward. With the right investments in education, training, and innovation, we can ensure that Africa's youth are ready to meet the challenges of tomorrow and build a prosperous, united continent.

We need to see these things:

- Comprehensive skills development programs
- Investment in education
- Support for vocational training and apprenticeships
- Lifelong learning opportunities

We can achieve this through the following:

- Public–private partnerships
- Expanding digital education platforms
- Creating innovation hubs and incubators
- Establishing skills farms

Public–Private Partnerships

We should leverage the strengths of both the public and private sectors to create more effective and responsive education and training programs. Companies can provide insights into the skills needed in the workforce, while governments can ensure that education policies align with these needs. Companies can also provide on-the-job training to get people into work quickly.

Expanding Digital Education Platforms

Digital platforms can deliver education across vast distances and to diverse populations and need to be central to an African-wide education strategy. We should expand access to online learning resources to ensure that those in remote areas have access to develop skills.

Creating Innovation Hubs and Incubators

We must establish hubs where ideas can be developed, tested, and brought to market. Such incubators would nurture young start-ups and provide resources, mentorship, and access to capital, enabling the next generation of African innovators to take the lead in shaping the future.

Establishing Skills Farms

Skills Farms would be like universities reimagined, whereby young people can get the skills they require in double time, massively shortcutting the time it normally takes to get a degree or vocational qualification.

HARNESSING YOUTH LEADERSHIP

We must harness youth leadership for today and for the future. Harnessing youth leadership is not just about preparing the next generation of leaders; it's about recognizing the leadership that already exists and providing these young people with the opportunities and platforms they need to lead.

We need to see these things:

- Youth-led initiatives and organizations gaining prominence
- Greater representation of young leaders in government and business
- Access to leadership training and mentorship programs for the youth
- Platforms for youth to influence policy and decision-making
- A safer environment for aspiring youth leaders and activists alike

We can achieve this through the following:

- Establishing youth councils and advisory boards
- Investing in leadership development programs for young people
- Creating mentorship networks that connect young leaders with experienced professionals

Establishing Youth Councils and Advisory Boards

Youth councils and advisory boards should operate locally, regionally, nationally, and continentally, providing young people with a direct platform to influence policy. By involving youth in formal structures, we can ensure that their voices are heard.

Investing in Leadership Development Programs

To prepare Africa's youth for leadership roles, we must invest in leadership development programs, which encourage critical skills such as strategic thinking, communication, negotiation, and ethics.

Mentorship

By connecting young leaders with experienced professionals, we can provide guidance, support, and valuable insights that help young people navigate the complexities of leadership.

All of these activities can be started today. None of them need heavy investment in infrastructure; none need substantial new investment or foreign involvement; none need development loans. All of these are things that African governments can start investing in testing and trialing today. While some of these initiatives may develop into large-scale operations, they can all start small. I believe they can all start now.

CODA: MOVING FORWARD

If not us, then who is going to take responsibility for uniting Africa in our lifetimes? If not us, then who is going to accelerate the lofty development plans we'd all like to see, by starting small, engaging the youth, and creating our future today?

I applaud any effort to define a better future for Africa, so in my conclusion, I want to loop back to the beginning, to where I started this journey, looking at the far-out vision of the 2063 agenda and asking myself, "Why should this take so long?"

Why indeed should we have to wait? Why should my generation and the generation after me see little or no benefit at all? Why, when we need to ask the youth of today to create this vision of the future, shouldn't they benefit? And why can't we get started more quickly, right here, right now?

We need to move forward, yet I sense stagnation. At best, I sense dragging feet, and at worst, I sense total paralysis, when leaders are simply treading water, afraid to upset the most volatile of status quos. I see other leaders working effectively to drive change, bringing prosperity where they can to the people they serve. I see good intentions, hard work, and hope. But I don't see enough action.

I don't pretend to have all the answers, but like so many of my fellow Africans, I do have plenty of ideas. We all have similar ideas around how we'd like to see Africa prosper. We all want to see her grow and flourish.

In this book I've outlined many scenarios for great change, and I, like the authors of Agenda 2063 and other plans for the continent's development, am under no illusion that implementing massive shifts doesn't take time, effort, and investment of huge proportion. Africa undoubtedly needs huge investment, effort, and time to get where she is going.

But Africa also needs small changes, incremental improvements, and mere tweaks to help start the shift. We need to start today with the things we can control. We do not have the luxury to wait until tomorrow.

So, I invite you, join me with your grand ambitions, your wild hopes and dreams for Africa. Then join me in thinking smaller, in thinking shorter term, in looking nearer, in looking within. Instead of waiting for a miracle, for extraordinary levels of investment from China, Russia, or elsewhere, instead of relying on the IMF, we should ask ourselves, "What can we do today?" and "How can we collaborate?"

By starting small we can work with our current resources. We can engage and harness youthful energy and optimism. We can build skills, we can become transparent, we can measure and track our progress, and we can enable new leaders.

In moving from a divided Africa to a united one, there's much to do, starting with empowering and engaging Africa's youth. I've outlined some of the answers, put forward the ideas, suggested the strategy. Now we just need to do it.

APPENDICES

In my research for this book I have learned so much about Africa, but also about the rest of the world. While we can of course learn from within, it is also important to look elsewhere, and so as in the appendices I share my thoughts on three mind-blowing concepts: the experiment of the United Arab Emirates, Nigeria as the key to Africa's success, and a case study on moonshot technology projects that could create a radical difference for our continent. These ideas offer us possibility; they show us that anything can be done.

THE EXPERIMENT: THE UAE

If you think organizing and aligning multiple nation-states together, building infrastructure, growing cities and industries, opening up for global trade, and making a name for yourself on the global stage is far-fetched or impossible, think again. Think about the United Arab Emirates.

I've spent time in the UAW, mainly for work, but I've enjoyed my time there. It is an optimistic, vibrant place of great opportunity. What is stunning about the place is its newness. The UAE was established in 1971. While the UAE is not Africa, does not have the same history as Africa, and does not have the same people or resources, I believe Africa can learn from, or be inspired by, the UAE, not least as an example of "doing a lot in a short amount of time." Indeed, what it has achieved is awe inspiring.

While the UAE is very much not an experiment, it is a vibrant successful country. As outsiders, we may view it as such when it comes to developing an African strategy. The UAE has done much of what Africa needs to do, what Africa can do. So, we can view the UAE as an experiment to learn from. We can learn from what has clearly worked. We can learn lessons and borrow from the best.

The UAE came into existence on December 2, 1971, marking the unification of the Trucial States, which were individual sheikhdoms that had been under British protection since the nineteenth century. The UAE initially comprised Abu Dhabi, Dubai, Sharjah, Ajman, Umm Al-Quwain, and Fujairah, with Ras Al Khaimah joining in 1972. The union was largely driven by the vision of Sheikh Zayed bin Sultan Al Nahyan of Abu Dhabi and Sheikh Rashid bin Saeed Al Maktoum of Dubai, who recognized the potential for greater economic and political stability.

The discovery and exploitation of oil in the twentieth century transformed the UAE's economy. Oil revenues fueled extensive infrastructure projects and modernization. Today, the UAE stands as a testament to rapid development, guided by visionary leadership and strategic investments.

The UAE is a federal absolute monarchy, with each of the seven emirates governed by its own monarch. The president of the UAE is traditionally the ruler of Abu Dhabi, while the prime minister is the ruler of Dubai. The Federal National Council (FNC) serves as an advisory body and is partly elected, reflecting gradual steps toward increased political participation.

Investment in world-class infrastructure has been the cornerstone of the UAE's development. The country boasts modern airports in Dubai and Abu Dhabi, serving as major international hubs, and an extensive road network complemented by metro systems and plans for high-speed rail. Iconic architectural feats like the Burj Khalifa, Burj Al Arab, and numerous luxury hotels and resorts underscore the UAE's commitment to being a global leader in construction and tourism. Jebel Ali in Dubai is the largest man-made harbor in the world, establishing the UAE as a leading port and logistics center in the Middle East.

Anyone who has visited the UAE can't fail to have been impressed by the scale and quality of its infrastructure, architecture, and opportunities for tourism, commerce, and business. It is thriving and wealthy. Nowhere else in the world have I seen so many luxury cars, so much wealth, yet so little crime. When I visit, I feel both safer than I do in the US or Europe and more inspired than I do anywhere. The very spectacle of Dubai or Abu Dhabi makes you believe that anything's possible. Imagine world-class services and infrastructure. Now imagine that none of it existed fifty years ago.

The UAE's health care and education have seen significant investments, resulting in advanced medical facilities and educational institutions, including branches of international universities. Some of the world's best educational institutions now also have franchises in the UAE. The British private schools Harrow School and Wellington College bring Harrow International School and the GEMS Wellington International School, which follow the British curriculum. New York University, the European Institute of Business Administration (INSEAD), and the Sorbonne (Paris) have established universities in Abu Dhabi.

The public school system in the UAE is robust and well developed, with a strong emphasis on providing quality education to all its citizens. Education is free and compulsory for all UAE nationals, from the six through twelfth grade.

Public schools in the UAE follow a national curriculum set by the Ministry of Education with an emphasis on Arabic language and Islamic studies, alongside core subjects such as mathematics, science, and English. There has been a strong push in recent years to align the education system with international standards, incorporating modern teaching methods and technology. These public schools also strive to be inclusive, providing education for students with special needs through dedicated programs and resources. Additionally, while the primary focus is on Emirati students, some public schools also admit expatriate students, although these students usually pay fees.

After completing secondary education, students can pursue higher education at numerous universities and colleges in the

UAE, many of which are public institutions offering free or subsidized education for Emiratis. The government also offers scholarships for students to study abroad.

Economic diversification has been key for the UAE in reducing its dependence on oil. The tourism sector has seen huge investments and has flourished with the development of luxury hotels, theme parks, and shopping malls, attracting millions of visitors each year.

Financial centers like the Dubai International Financial Centre have positioned the UAE as a global financial hub. Significant investments in technology parks and smart city initiatives demonstrate a commitment to innovation and sustainable development. In turn, investment in business has seen the UAE attract a growing numbers of expats, both to work in global businesses and to set up start-ups. The UAE has become a magnet for global business and investment, thanks to its numerous free zones that offer great conditions for foreign investors.

While previously businesses in the UAE were required to be at least 51 percent owned by Emiratis, 100 percent foreign ownership is now possible; this has attracted many businesses to the region. I myself have established a business in the UAE because of the appealing business environment. The country consistently ranks high in global indices for ease of doing business and is positioned well to act as a strategic hub between the East and West.

So, it's a land of opportunity, but what is it like to live there? I was struck not only by how good life looks for Emirates, but how so many diverse expats from all over the world are drawn to the UAE; indeed expats make up between 85 to 90 percent of the population. Expats come from South Asia, including India, Pakistan, Bangladesh, and Sri Lanka; North America; Europe; Arab nations, including Egypt, Jordan, and Lebanon; and Asian countries, including the Philippines, China, and South Korea. Additionally, they relocate from African nations, including Nigeria, Kenya, and South Africa. Expats tend to work across various sectors, including construction, health care, finance, technology, and hospitality, and contribute to economic growth and cultural diversity in dynamic, cosmopolitan cities.

Nowhere is without problems or challenges The UAE has seen rapid growth and has needed to bring in migrant workers to fuel that expansion. In the rush to build new buildings and infrastructure, some workers died in the extreme working conditions of forty- to fifty-degree Celsius heat. While the UAE has taken steps toward improving workers' rights, significant challenges remain. The UAE's labor system, known as the kafala system, ties migrant workers' legal status to their employers, making it difficult for workers to change jobs or leave the country without the employer's permission. This has been criticized for being open to abuse.

Women still face some challenges. Personal status laws, often based on Islamic Sharia law, favor men, particularly in matters of marriage and divorce. Inheritance laws are also imbalanced, with women typically receiving half the inheritance of their male counterparts. The UAE has made progress in relaxing some guardianship rules, yet women may still need a male guardian's consent for certain activities. At work, like in many countries, women may face inequality in hiring, promotions, and pay, and maternity policies can be less generous compared to international standards. The UAE government has taken steps to improve women's rights and participation. Initiatives to boost female representation in government and business sectors and support women's entrepreneurship and professional development are underway. Plus, many business initiatives now aim to attract women to the workforce in the UAE, including schemes to attract and support women-led businesses.

Notwithstanding issues for workers and women, it's impossible to ignore the enormous achievement of the UAE. In just over fifty years, the UAE has grown from disparate states in the desert to a global player. Geopolitically, the UAE has cemented its influence through participation in global affairs and adopting the outward-in approach of attracting investment, trade, and tourism.

As I mentioned, I've visited the UAE mainly for work, and what is most striking as a visitor is just how rich the place is. Money and wealth are everywhere. Most people enjoy a very high quality of life, and that makes sense when you look at the relative GDP of the UAE. The GDP per capita (GDPPC) in the

UAE is $96,000, which sits above US's $85,000. For comparison, Libya is the African country with the highest GDPPC at $26,000, Botswana's GDP per capita is $20,000, South Africa's is $16,000, Ghana's is $7,000, and Nigeria's is $6,000. At the other end of the scale in Africa, the Central African Republic's GDPPC is $1,100 and the Republic of South Sudan's is just $455.[79]

Masdar City: The City of the Future

Masdar City[80] is not as famous as Dubai or Abu Dhabi; indeed, it sits on the edge of Abu Dhabi as a pioneering urban development project: the city of tomorrow. Launched in 2006 by the Abu Dhabi Future Energy Company, the project aims to be one of the world's most sustainable urban communities and pitches itself as "sustainable living made easy."

And it looks good too: Its architecture incorporates traditional Arabic design with modern sustainable practices. Buildings are strategically aligned to maximize natural light and ventilation while minimizing heat gain, reducing the need for air conditioning. Energy efficiency is a core principle, resulting in lower energy consumption. Solar is, of course, a primary energy source, with one of the largest solar panel arrays in the Middle East providing much of the city's energy needs.

Transport is innovative and environmentally friendly. The Personal Rapid Transit (PRT) system features driverless electric vehicles that transport residents and visitors around the city, reducing reliance on cars and lowering emissions. The city is also pedestrian friendly, with shaded walkways and pedestrian areas. Advanced water management systems reduce consumption through gray water recycling and efficient irrigation for landscaping.

Around 5,000 people live in the city, and it is a magnet for innovative businesses. It has already attracted over 600

---

79 https://www.imf.org/external/datamapper/PPPPC@WEO/OEMDC/ADVEC/WEOWORLD

80 https://www.masdarcity.ae

businesses though its free zone and attractive setup offers, including start-ups, research institutions, and multinationals. Notably, 30 percent of these businesses are led by women, highlighting the city's support for female entrepreneurship and leadership.

Masdar City is a bold experiment in urban sustainability and shows a glimpse of cities of the future. I would love to see cities like Masdar in Africa.

What's next for the UAE?

UAE Centennial 2071[81] is an ambitious long-term vision and strategy "to ensure the UAE's future prosperity." This plan is designed to honor the country's hundred-year birthday and captures the UAE's aspirations to be among the best countries in the world. It focuses on four key pillars: education, economy, government development, and community cohesion.

At its core is the transformation of the education system. The UAE aims to create a world-class educational framework that prepares its young people for future challenges and opportunities. It will integrate advanced technology, foster creativity and critical thinking, and emphasize scientific research and innovation. The goal is to cultivate a generation of highly skilled professionals and leaders who can drive the nation's progress and sustain its global competitive edge.

Economic diversification and sustainability are also key. The plan includes a shift from an oil-based economy to a knowledge-based one. Investments in renewable energy, AI, and space exploration are key. The UAE wishes to establish itself as a global hub for trade, finance, and tourism.

Government efficiency and effectiveness will be improved by adopting innovative governance models and smart technologies.

[81] https://u.ae/en/about-the-uae/strategies-initiatives-and-awards/strategies-plans-and-visions/innovation-and-future-shaping/uae-centennial-2071

They will improve public services, promote transparency, and foster a culture of continuous improvement.

Creating an inclusive society is a key priority. The plan promotes tolerance, happiness, and well-being among citizens and residents. Initiatives are designed to enhance social welfare and ensure a high quality of life for all.

To achieve these ambitious goals, UAE Centennial 2071 outlines a series of strategic projects and initiatives across various sectors and encourages collaboration among government entities, the private sector, and international partners. The 2071 plan is not as far as the UAE can see, however. Hugely ambitious and forward thinking is its "moonshot" project Mars 2117, as the UAE aims to establish the first inhabitable human settlement in Mars by 2117.[82]

Could this be Africa?

If the ingredients of this rapid success are rich natural resources, talented people, a willingness to collaborate and "be more than the sum of its parts," economic diversification, and inward investment, could Africa emulate the UAE and do something similar? Could Africa do something equally transformative? Well, I think yes: Africa can do this by drawing valuable lessons from the UAE's rapid development.

One of the UAE's most significant achievements is diversification of the economy beyond oil. African countries, many of which are heavily reliant on a single commodity or sector, could benefit from developing more diverse economic sectors, for example, tourism, technology, finance, and renewable energy. By reducing dependence on a single industry, they can become more resilient.

---

[82] https://u.ae/eu/about-the-uae/strategies-initiatives-and-awards/strategies-plans-and-visions/innovation-and-future-shaping/uae-centennial-2071

The UAE has invested in robust infrastructure, including transport, telecoms, and health care. African nations could prioritize similar investments to improve connectivity, access to services, and overall productivity. High-quality infrastructure, in turn, attracts outside investment and facilitates growth. By creating a business-friendly environment, the UAE has stimulated growth. African countries could improve regulatory frameworks, reduce bureaucracy, and provide incentives to attract and retain investment. Borrowing the economic free zones idea would also spur economic growth.

The UAE's strong emphasis on education and health care recognizes that a healthy, educated population is crucial for sustainable development. I strongly believe Africa should create unified health and education systems to ensure populations are equipped with the skills and well-being needed to prosper. The UAE's political stability has been a key factor in its economic success. This is where Africa has a long way to go. African nations should work toward ensuring political stability and good governance. Reducing corruption is a first step in this direction for some African nations. Increasing political stability must come first.

The UAE has embraced innovation and technology, establishing itself as a hub for technology start-ups and innovative enterprises. African countries should invest in technology and innovation, promoting entrepreneurship and creating environments that encourage the growth of innovative industries. Africa will need to find the sectors that make sense for Africa. An investment in education could support a focus on defense technology and cybersecurity, allowing Africa to become the powerhouse of peacekeeping, globally. The UAE has launched several initiatives focused on sustainability and renewable energy, a prime example of which is Masdar City. African nations, many of which face environmental challenges, could prioritize sustainable development, invest in renewables, and build cities of the future.

Tourism has been a success for the UAE, and it hosts tourists from all around the world. African countries, rich in natural beauty and cultural heritage, could enhance their tourism infrastructure, market their attractions globally, and create policies that make it easier for tourists to visit. Africa has so much to offer in this regard, yet few see Africa as a top tourist destination.

The UAE has created public–private partnerships to fund and manage large-scale infrastructure and development projects. I would like to see more such partnerships developed in Africa to support much needed infrastructure development, albeit with a diverse set of commercial partners, coming from a range of markets. The UAE's long-term strategic plans, such as Centennial 2071, have set clear goals for national development. I believe a clear vision for the future would help Africa achieve similar success.

It might be easy to jump to the conclusion that Africa, with its relatively low GDPPC, cannot rise to the level of the UAE in terms of development or wealth. However, it's important to remember the UAE simply didn't exist sixty years ago. And while it's GDP grew through oil, it was only $15,000 in the 1980s. The 1990s saw its GDPPC grow further to $25,000, *after* significant investment in infrastructure. And while much of its development was kickstarted by oil, its GDP has grown significantly due to its diversification away from being an oil-based economy; in the 2000s it climbed to $45,000 after other sectors took off. If Africa can harness its own resources to kickstart its growth, and then keep going, there's no reason it could not achieve something similar.

NIGERIA: THE KEY TO AFRICA'S SUCCESS

I feel strongly that all of Africa must unite, but first there are strategic and structural challenges that need to be overcome. Nigeria, known to many in the world as the "Giant of Africa," is a vital linchpin in Africa's success. With its vast resources, dynamic population, and strategic position, Nigeria holds a critical role in shaping the continent's future. With Nigeria's significant influence, the country's trajectory will have a profound impact on the broader African landscape.

Here, I explore why we all need Nigeria to thrive if Africa as a whole is to thrive. Some might say Nigeria is already thriving, with the largest economic output and population in Africa, but I want to look at two problems facing Nigeria: insurgency and corruption. I fear, as many do, that unless these two issues are solved, Nigeria cannot truly grasp its potential and, as such, cannot fully support Africa's development.

First is a little background for the uninitiated. Nigeria is strategically positioned in West Africa, sharing borders with four countries: Benin to the west, Niger to the north, Chad to the northeast, and Cameroon to the east. To the south, it has a coastline along the Gulf of Guinea in the Atlantic Ocean. Nigeria's geographic location makes it a significant player in regional politics and economics, serving as a gateway between West Africa and the rest of the continent.

Nigeria is not the biggest country in Africa in terms of geography; no, it gets its "Giant of Africa" nickname from its population size. Nigeria boasts approximately 15 percent[83] of the continent's total population. With over 200 million people, it is by far the most populous country in Africa. Like much of Africa, Nigeria's population is young, with a median age of around eighteen years, offering huge potential for a substantial workforce in coming decades. While countries like Egypt and South Africa also boast large economies, Nigeria's population size gives it a unique edge in terms of market potential and workforce. Nigeria's population growth is spurred by its high fertility rate with an average of 5.7 children per woman.

Economically, Nigeria stands out as one of Africa's largest economies. Its GDP, estimated at $1.279 trillion,[84] is among the highest on the continent, often competing closely with South Africa for the top position, which in 2023 generated $1.277 trillion.[85] Its GDP is significantly higher than that of neighboring countries like Ghana and Cameroon. By 2050, Nigeria is

[83] https://en.wikipedia.org/wiki/List_of_African_countries_by_population

[84] https://www.worldeconomics.com/Country-Size/South Africa.aspx

[85] https://www.worldeconomics.com/Country-Size/Nigeria.aspx

projected to be the fifteenth largest economy in the world and is set to overtake Italy, Spain, and Canada.[86]

Nigeria's economy is heavily reliant on its oil and gas sector, which constitutes a significant portion of its GDP and export revenues. The country is one of the largest oil producers in Africa, and its oil reserves rank among the highest globally.

Let's just dwell on that for a minute. Nigeria's oil reserves actually rank tenth (or eleventh) in the world depending on data variances. It has 37 billion barrels of oil in reserve—more than the US. The UAE has more, at 98 billion barrels, and is the seventh largest reserve in the world. At the top is not Saudi Arabia, with 259 billion barrels, or Iran, with 209 billion barrels, but interestingly Venezuela with a staggering potential wealth of 304 billion barrels in reserve.[87]

If you have read my thoughts on how the UAE could act as a relevant and poignant experiment or example of how to leverage natural resources to build great economic opportunity quickly, and think Africa doesn't have the resources, think again. Africa, specifically Nigeria, is incredibly resource rich.

In terms of regional influence, Nigeria is a leading member of the Economic Community of West African States (ECOWAS) and plays a critical role in shaping regional policies and initiatives. Its large market makes it a central hub for trade and investment in West Africa. The country's influence extends beyond economics: Culturally, it is a powerhouse, with Nollywood, its film industry, being one of the largest in the world. While Nigeria can claim to be a successful country, there are some large issues that really hold its people back and, in turn, limit the standing of Nigeria on the world stage. A high poverty rate, income inequality, and a lack of key infrastructure are the symptoms of larger issues.

86 https://www.theworldcounts.com/populations/countries/nigeria

87 https://en.wikipedia.org/wiki/List_of_countries_by_proven_oil_reserves

The problem of corruption

Sadly, I need to focus in on corruption. For readers who aren't familiar with this issue, you may imagine small- to medium-scale or sporadic issues, for example, a government occasionally finding itself in the pocket of multinationals or some occasional local vote rigging. Sadly, this would be wishful thinking. Corruption in Nigeria is a pervasive and deeply rooted issue that affects nearly every aspect of society. The problem is not just serious; it is systemic, influencing the political, economic, and social fabric of the nation. Nigeria consistently ranks poorly on global corruption indices,[88] indicating the severity and widespread nature of the issue.

Politically, corruption manifests in the form of bribery, embezzlement of public funds, and electoral fraud. High-profile cases often involve government officials and politicians who siphon vast amounts of public money for personal gain. Former governors and ministers have been prosecuted for corruption, although the success rate of these prosecutions is low, due, in part, to a compromised judicial system. The political elite often use their positions to get rich at the expense of the people, perpetuating a cycle of impunity and a disappointing lack of accountability.

Economically, of course, corruption severely hampers development. Public funds that should be invested in infrastructure, health care, education, and other essential services are often diverted. Misallocation of resources leads to poor services and underdevelopment.

Socially, corruption erodes trust in public institutions. When people believe that their leaders are corrupt, it diminishes faith in the government and its ability to serve the public. Everyday corruption, such as the need to pay bribes for basic services, further entrenches poverty and inequality. Ordinary Nigerians face extortion in schools, hospitals, and other public services, creating a culture in which corruption is sadly normalized—and it's everywhere.

---

[88] https://www.transparency.org/en/cpi/2023/index/nga

The oil sector, which is the backbone of Nigeria's economy, is particularly plagued by corruption. Oil revenues, which could contribute to supporting radical development in Nigeria and beyond, and could potentially lift millions out of poverty, frequently disappear into the pockets of a few. The nation's vast oil wealth remains largely untapped for public benefit.

The impact of corruption on Nigeria's development is profound. It stifles economic growth by deterring foreign investment, as, expectedly, investors are wary of the unpredictable business environment and the additional costs associated with corrupt practices. Corruption also exacerbates poverty and inequality, as resources meant for development are misappropriated. It undermines the effectiveness of public institutions, making it difficult for the government to implement policies and deliver public goods efficiently.

Things simply don't get done. Development simply can't happen.

Despite efforts to combat corruption, progress has been slow. Anti-corruption agencies like the Economic and Financial Crimes Commission[89] (EFCC) are working toward their mission to "eradicate economic and financial crimes through prevention, enforcement and coordination." High-profile convictions are rare, and when they occur, they often result in light sentences—really light sentences.

For example, if you look at the convictions of the EFCC,[90] you can see, for starters, that most are small scale and that they result in optional sentences, that is, either a prison term or a fine. Scanning down the list of sentences reveals an odd picture: Many are for three, six, or nine months *or* a fine of between ₦ 200,000 to ₦ 500,000. And, of course, when offered a choice, as most are, no one does jail time. You can see why, as ₦ 200,000 is about $130 at the time of writing this book. It seems that even when guilty of corruption charges, it is still possible to pay your way out of it.

---

[89] https://www.efcc.gov.ng/efcc/

[90] https://www.efcc.gov.ng/efcc/images/pdfs/3785_Convictions_recorded_in_2022.pdf

The EFCC is not without controversy; a look at its own website reveals it is sharing information on some of its own former staffers on its wanted persons' page. The site warns users that these former employees are "no longer a staff of the Economic and Financial Crimes Commission (EFCC) and have no authority to represent it or carry out any business in the name of the Commission"[91]—not a shining indictment.

There have been many other reports of EFCC officials engaging in corrupt practices, such as accepting bribes to drop cases or manipulating investigations for personal gain. Such allegations undermine the credibility of the commission and cast doubt on its ability to effectively combat corruption.

Operational inefficiencies and legal challenges are reported to have further complicated the EFCC's work. The commission has faced criticism for its methods of investigation, which some have described as heavy handed. There have also been instances when high-profile cases prosecuted by the EFCC have ended in acquittals due to lack of evidence or procedural errors, reflecting poorly on the commission's effectiveness and preparedness.

The leadership of the EFCC has also been a source of controversy. For instance, in 2020, Ibrahim Magu, then acting chairman of the EFCC, was arrested and suspended amid allegations of corruption and insubordination. An investigative panel was set up to probe the accusations against him, which included the mismanagement of recovered assets and insubordination to the Office of the Attorney General. The investigation and subsequent suspension highlighted significant issues within the agency's leadership and operation: "14 fraud cases involving N118 billion and $309 million were abandoned by the anti-graft commission under his watch."[92]

In May 2024, it was claimed that the EFCC released a list of fifty-eight ex-governors accused of looting over N2 trillion in

[91] https://www.efcc.gov.ng/efcc/news-and-information/wanted-persons-1

[92] https://punchng.com/n118bn-309m-fraud-cases-concealed-under-magu-panel/

public funds. Then the EFCC denied the list had anything to do with them. The list went viral on social media, but fact-checked sources[93] suggest the list did not in fact come from EFCC. Who would spread disinformation about widespread corruption?

So many of the challenges I see in Africa are linked, and this is a prime example. While I do not pretend to know whether the list of ex-governors under investigation is true or false or, if false, who is spreading disinformation, it provides a solid case study. Viral dis- or misinformation (if this is what this is) has the potential to cause significant civil dissatisfaction, mistrust, and, potentially, civil unrest. It is in the interest of some to cause unrest, or at least instability, to prevent African nations from developing a more stable leadership. Some who might do that sit within Africa; others sit far away. Skills in cybersecurity will allow Africans to verify information quickly and know whether they are looking at a large corruption issue or a large disinformation issue. Both are bad news for Africa. We must clean up corruption, and we certainly can't allow corruption to be used as a weapon to cause unrest.

Addressing corruption

When a problem is entrenched, addressing it requires a multi-faceted approach. It seems hard, yet it is possible. Strengthening institutions, ensuring the independence of the judiciary, and enhancing transparency and accountability in government operations can all go a long way to ending, or at least reducing, corruption. Civil society and the media also play crucial roles in holding officials accountable and advocating for reform.

Addressing corruption requires comprehensive reforms, strong institutions, and a collective effort from both the government and the public to create a culture of accountability and integrity. Addressing the challenge of corruption is crucial for Nigeria to fully harness its potential and reinforce its position as a key player in Africa's development. Addressing corruption will also end the conditions that allow insurgency to take hold.

[93] https://africacheck.org/fact-checks/meta-programme-fact-checks/no-nigerias-financial-crimes-agency-didnt-release-list-58-ex

Insurgency

If corruption is typified by using political office for personal gain, then insurgency might appear to some as a radical solution to systemic issues. Indeed, insurgents such as Boko Haram even cite corruption as just cause for murder and kidnapping. However, insurgency rarely results in full-scale revolution and more often leads to pervasive destabilization that harms societies. This destabilization disrupts lives, economies, and governance, creating a cycle of violence and poverty. To illustrate these points, I want to explore the problems of insurgency through the lens of Nigeria, focusing on the activities of the Muslim insurgent group Boko Haram and its impact on education, on women and girls, and on the wider society in Nigeria.

In 2014, 276 schoolgirls were kidnapped from a school in Chibok by Boko Haram. It brought global attention to the group's brutality and the Nigerian government's struggle to combat terrorism. The immediate impact was a heightened sense of insecurity, not just in Nigeria but globally, as it showcased the reach and ruthlessness of extremist groups. The girls were held in a camp, some forced to "marry" (they were raped), and some bearing children in captivity. More than 180 have either been freed or escaped in the ten years since. The rest, some 112,[94] are still unaccounted for.

The abduction severely disrupted education in the region, as many parents, fearing similar attacks, withdrew their daughters from school. This response disrupted education for many thousands more as this setback in girls' education further entrenched gender inequalities. Families were torn apart, with many parents enduring years of anguish over the fate of their daughters. The psychological trauma for the girls who escaped or were eventually released is immense, with many requiring extensive support to recover from their ordeal, with many unhappy with the support they have been given by the Nigerian government.[95] But that is just the tip of the iceberg.

[94] https://bringbackourgirls.ng/

[95] https://www.bbc.co.uk/news/world-africa-68769102

In a wider context, the insurgency and its impact on education highlight the failure of governance to address corruption and inequality, demonstrating the dire consequences for the most vulnerable populations. Economically, the instability has deterred investment and development in northern Nigeria, exacerbating poverty and unemployment. By examining this in a little more depth, I want to better understand the complex interplay between corruption, insurgency, and the quest for stability and development in Nigeria.

The Muslim insurgency in West Africa, particularly driven by groups such as Boko Haram and the Islamic State in West Africa Province (ISWAP), has had profound and devastating impacts on the region. Boko Haram, which translates to "Western education is forbidden," emerged in northeastern Nigeria in the early 2000s. Initially focused on opposing Western education and values, the group evolved into a violent jihadist organization aiming to establish an Islamic state governed by Sharia law. While it is globally notorious for the girls' kidnapping, Boko Haram's insurgency has resulted in far more harms. The group's tactics include attacking civilians, schools, mosques, churches, and government installations. It has also carried out suicide bombings and used improvised explosive devices (IEDs). It is responsible for tens of thousands of deaths and has displaced millions of people, primarily in Nigeria, but also in neighboring countries like Niger, Chad, and Cameroon.

ISWAP, a splinter group from Boko Haram, formed in 2016 after internal disagreements within Boko Haram's leadership. It aligned itself with the Islamic State (ISIS) and has since gained notoriety for its strategic and brutal attacks, particularly targeting military and government installations, as well as civilian populations.

The roots of the insurgency lie in deep-seated socioeconomic issues. Many parts of West Africa, especially the regions where these groups are most active, suffer from extreme poverty, lack of education, and limited economic opportunities. For instance, in northern Nigeria, where Boko Haram has been most active, the poverty rate exceeds 70 percent, and literacy levels are significantly lower than in the southern regions of the country.

High unemployment rates, especially among young people, create a fertile ground for extremist recruitment. Insurgents exploit these vulnerabilities, offering money, a sense of belonging, and promises of a better life.

The Nigerian government, with support from neighboring countries and international partners, has launched military offensives to combat the group. The Multinational Joint Task Force (MNJTF), comprising troops from Nigeria, Chad, Cameroon, Niger, and Benin, has been instrumental in reclaiming territory from Boko Haram. Military operations have often also been supported by international partners such as the United States and France. Despite Nigeria's strategy to involve its neighbors and take a regional approach, the group remains a significant threat, continuing to carry out attacks and posing a persistent security challenge.

While military efforts are necessary in the fight against insurgency, effective development is crucial too. Development programs aimed at addressing the underlying socioeconomic issues will go a long way to stopping insurgency in its tracks. One example of a holistic approach is the Lake Chad Basin Commission's Regional Stabilization Strategy,[96] which aims to restore security and facilitate development in the areas affected by Boko Haram. This strategy is focused on rebuilding infrastructure, providing education, and creating job opportunities to address the conditions that fuel insurgency.

One thing is for sure, and it's that corruption, inadequate security forces, and ineffective government responses have created fertile ground for insurgency, and it will take strong leadership, holistic development, and the eradication of corruption to successfully combat it. Nigeria has the potential to win the fight against insurgency by leveraging regional partnerships and by tackling its own internal corruption issues. I know I am not the only one who understands these topics are inextricably linked and that they must be tackled together.

---

[96] https://www.undp.org/africa/regional-stabilization-facility-lake-chad-basin

Africa needs Nigeria to thrive

Nigeria's successes or failures, indeed Nigeria's problems and opportunities, inevitably ripple across Africa. If Nigeria thrives, it can serve as a powerful engine for regional development, driving economic growth, innovation, and stability. Conversely, if Nigeria struggles, it risks dragging down the continent's prospects due to its interconnectedness with other African economies.

Politically, Nigeria's stability is crucial for Africa. As one of the continent's largest democracies, Nigeria has the potential to be a model for governance and political stability.

Education and infrastructure are other key areas where Nigeria needs support. A well-educated population is essential for economic development and innovation. By investing in education, Nigeria can harness the potential of its young population, turning it into a demographic dividend rather than a burden.

A key strategy for supporting Nigeria involves enhancing regional integration. Nigeria is a cornerstone of the Economic Community of West African States (ECOWAS) and can play a pivotal role in advancing regional trade and cooperation. By removing trade barriers, improving cross-border infrastructure, and simplifying regulations, ECOWAS can create a more integrated and competitive regional market. I would be keen to see further integration and removal of trade barriers across Africa.

Economic growth must be inclusive, ensuring that the benefits reach all segments of society. This requires targeted policies that support marginalized communities, create job opportunities, and provide social safety nets. By reducing inequality and lifting people out of poverty, Nigeria can build a more cohesive and stable society, which is conducive to sustainable development.

From a strategic perspective, international partnerships are crucial. Nigeria's allies, including Western countries and emerging powers, have a role to play in its development. Multinationals have a huge role to play in the country's development and the development of consumers; however, the country must remain stable for it to offer a suitable environment in which to do business.

Nigeria's woes have sadly caused it to lose several multinationals in recent months. While the middle class in Nigeria is on the rise, inflation has meant that consumers are no longer buying, and devaluation has meant the cost of doing business in the country is growing exponentially.

On March 17, 2023, Unilever Nigeria announced[97] it was discontinuing production of its home care and skin care brands, including Omo, Sunlight, and Lux. However, Unilever will continue to operate its other verticals in Nigeria.

On August 3, 2023, GSK (Glaxo Smithkline) announced "it plans to stop doing business after evaluating the options for moving to a third-party distribution model for its drugs and consumer healthcare goods." GSK Nigeria, which has faced increased competition from local companies and imports from India and China, said "its half-year sales had dropped to 7.75 billion naira ($9.82 million), from 14.8 billion naira in the same period a year ago."[98]

Kimberly-Clark announced[99] on May 31, 2024, that "it has made the difficult decision to exit its business in Nigeria after almost 15 years, due to recently refocused company strategic priorities globally as well as economic developments in the country. Kimberly-Clark will close its manufacturing facility and commercial office in Lagos and will no longer manufacture, market, or sell its Huggies and Kotex products in the country."

Ultimately, Nigeria's success is intertwined with Africa's success. The continent's future cannot be detached from Nigeria's trajectory. By supporting Nigeria in addressing its economic, political, and social challenges, the international community

---

[97] https://africa.businessinsider.com/local/markets/unilever-halts-sale-of-home-and-skin-care-products-gains-n81-billion-in-nine-months/w4nfft7

[98] https://www.reuters.com/business/healthcare-pharmaceuticals/gsk-nigeria-calls-an-end-its-business-return-cash-2023-08-03/#:~:text=ABUJA

[99] https://www.news.kimberly-clark.com/2024-05-31-Kimberly-Clark-To-Exit-Nigeria

and African neighbors can help unlock the country's potential. This, in turn, can drive broader African development, creating a more prosperous, stable, and integrated continent. The vision of a thriving Africa, with Nigeria at its core, is not just a hopeful aspiration but a strategic necessity.

CASE STUDY: CLOSING THE COMMUNICATION GAP

As I travel in Africa, I bring expectations from my life as a US and European citizen with me. While I expect many glorious differences when I'm in Africa, I always unrealistically seem to expect that communication is easy. And I'm always disappointed. In Africa, communication is still something that Africans can't take for granted, and it has a big impact on almost everything.

This is a problem for everyone, but especially for young people looking to develop their skills and careers. The promise of the global gig economy is tantalizing for many, offering opportunities to connect with clients and employers around the world, work flexibly, and earn globally competitive wages. However, many Africans struggle to fully participate in the digital marketplace due to poor internet connectivity.

Imagine a talented graphic designer in Kumasi, Ghana, eager to showcase her skills to a global audience. She registers on a freelancing platform like UpWork or Fiverr, uploads her portfolio, and starts attracting freelance projects. But, unlike her counterparts in Europe or North America, she faces the significant challenge of unreliable internet connectivity. Frequent power outages, slow speeds, and high costs make it difficult for her to communicate with clients, meet deadlines, and upload large files. This frustrating scenario is a reality for many Africans who aspire to join the online gig economy.

I've seen this firsthand at many levels. I am a great believer in the idea that technology can democratize work, can level the playing field for talent, and can drive dynamic global growth—but only if reliable connectivity is present. I've seen how entrepreneurial friends of mine have hired African freelancers or collaborated with African innovators and complain about the endless and sporadic, unpredictable interruption to their ability to attend meetings, to connect and share work. I fear that, for businesses looking to outsource work to Africa, the lack of reliable internet infrastructure can be a deterrent.

Africa Needs to Catch Up

What many Africans experience in terms of connectivity day to day is something many people care not to remember in the US and Europe; they're at least a decade ahead. Outside of the world of work, Africa's internet penetration rates, though improving, remain among the lowest in the world. Only about 43 percent of Africans had access to the internet as of 2021[100] compared to a global average of 66 percent. In many rural areas, connectivity is even scarcer, and where it is available, it is often prohibitively expensive and unreliable.

In some African countries, there is a booming tech-savvy population. Morocco (88 percent), Seychelles (82 percent), Tunisia (79 percent), Botswana (74 percent), and South Africa (72 percent) top the list in terms of internet penetration rates, whereas Uganda (10 percent), the DRC (9 percent), South Sudan (7 percent), Burundi (6 percent), and Somalia (2 percent) are at the bottom.[101] Even in relatively more connected countries, the infrastructure often lags behind the demand. Urban areas might have decent connectivity but move just a little way out into the suburbs or rural areas, and the situation changes drastically.

Investing in Radical Innovation

To address Africa's patchy connectivity, due to underinvestment and geographical issues, there have been various initiatives aimed at improving internet connectivity across the continent. Not all have been a success. You may have heard of Project Loon, an initiative by Google's parent company Alphabet Inc. It was

[100] https://www.statista.com/topics/9813/internet-usage-in-africa/
[101] https://data.worldbank.org/indicator/IT.NET.USER.ZS

designed to provide internet access to remote and underserved areas using high-altitude balloons. These balloons, equipped with specialized communication equipment, were deployed into the stratosphere, about twenty kilometers (twelve miles) above the Earth's surface, to create a network of floating cell towers.

The primary goal of Project Loon was to deliver internet connectivity to regions where traditional infrastructure was either too expensive or impractical to implement. This was especially relevant for rural and remote areas, as well as regions affected by natural disasters where existing communication networks might have been disrupted.

The operation of Project Loon was both innovative and complex. Each balloon was powered by solar panels and designed to stay aloft for extended periods, sometimes up to several months. The balloons were equipped with transceivers to communicate with ground stations and with each other, forming a mesh network that could deliver internet service directly to users' LTE-enabled devices. Using advanced AI, the balloons navigated by adjusting their altitude to catch winds moving in the desired direction, allowing them to stay in targeted areas or move as needed.

It faced several challenges, including technical issues related to balloon longevity and navigation and the high costs associated with maintaining and scaling the balloon fleet, plus regulatory issues. Additionally, as technology and terrestrial internet infrastructure continued to improve, the relative advantage of the balloon-based system diminished; it just became less necessary. Alphabet announced that it was shutting down Project Loon in January 2021, citing the project's inability to achieve a sustainable business model despite its significant and interesting technical achievements.

Furthermore, governments and private sector players are increasingly recognizing the importance of investing in internet infrastructure. Alphabet hasn't given up, not by a long shot. Google's Equiano cable, a subsea fiber-optic cable spanning 15,000 kilometers from Portugal to South Africa, has two landing points in Nigeria and Namibia. According to a study, "the

Equiano cable will increase connectivity more than fivefold in Nigeria and twofold in South Africa and Namibia. In addition, the study projects the creation of 1.6 million jobs between 2022 and 2025 in Nigeria, 180,000 in South Africa, and 21,000 in Namibia."[102]

As recently as May 2024, Google Cloud announced new investments in digital infrastructure and security initiatives designed to increase digital connectivity, accelerate economic growth, and deepen resilience across Africa. Umoja (meaning unity), is the first ever fiber optic route to directly connect Africa with Australia.[103]

Meta, also, is investing with 2Africa,[104] "the largest subsea fiber-optic cable system ever," and Elon Musk's SpaceX is deploying Starlink to many African countries within 2024. Starlink promises users can "engage in activities that have historically not been possible with satellite internet. Made possible via the world's largest constellation of highly advanced satellites operating in a low orbit around the Earth." [105]

Opportunism, Not Altruism

Big Tech investment in African connectivity infrastructure is on the rise, and understandably so. There is so much untapped wealth from connectivity. Connectivity can unlock all sorts of opportunities: from education to improved health care, to mobilizing a labor force, to enabling e-commerce and trade. But Silicon Valley investment is not without perceived problems. What happens if Californian ideals don't align with African values? Who is regulating data and AI? Why aren't African governments in control of their infrastructure?

---

[102] https://african.business/2023/07/technology-information/can-africa-achieve-digital-sovereignty-in-an-era-of-big-tech

[103] https://cloud.google.com/blog/products/infrastructure/investing-in-connectivity-and-growth-for-africa

[104] https://www.2africacable.net/

Beyond infrastructure, there are other systemic issues at play that have made connectivity and internet adoption rates difficult in Africa. The high costs of data and limited digital literacy also play their part. For many Africans, accessing the internet costs a significant portion of their income, making it a luxury rather than a utility. Even when connectivity is available, not everyone has the digital skills needed to benefit from a regional or global marketplace.

INDEX

ABOUT THE AUTHOR

Adu Opoku-Boahin is an author and business leader who has enjoyed a successful career as a strategy consultant, advising some of the world's most successful organizations on how to structure themselves, how to harness technology, how to attract and retain talent, and how to create great change. Deeply interested in global business and policies and the tectonic shifts made possible by technology, Adu employed his strategic skills when writing his second book, *Disrupting the African Mindset.*

Born in Africa, raised in Austria, and living in the United States, Adu increasingly works with African policymakers and has a unique perspective on both the potential and the challenges of the African continent. Adu wrote *Disrupting the African Mindset: From Divided to United* to share his vision for a united Africa.

Made in United States
North Haven, CT
31 July 2026

15479642R00163